SUPERFOODS 24/7

Delicious Recipes for Superfoods at Every Meal

First published in the UK in 2016 by
Apple Press
74–77 White Lion Street
London N1 9PF
United Kingdom

www.apple-press.com

ISBN: 9781845436186

Printed in China by 1010 Printing International Ltd.
9 8 7 6 5 4 3 2 1

This book was conceived, designed and produced by
Quantum Books Limited
6 Blundell Street
London N7 9BH
United Kingdom

Publisher: Kerry Enzor
Cover and text design: Lucy Parissi
Photographer: Jackie Sobon
Project editor: Rachel Malig
Assistant editor: Emma Harverson

QUMSF24

SUPERFOODS 24/7

Delicious Recipes for Superfoods at Every Meal

JESSICA NADEL

CONTENTS

INTRODUCING SUPERFOODS

THERE IS A REAL SUPERFOOD BUZZ IN THE AIR RIGHT NOW, and with so many of us looking for ways to better ourselves through lifestyle and diet, there is definitely good reason to become more attuned to what we're eating. I truly believe that there are some amazing and magical superfoods out there, which can promote health and vitality as part of a well-balanced diet.

So what do I consider to be superfoods? For me, they're whole, plant-based foods, *real* foods, that are thought to have additional health-supporting properties. Their main feature is that they are nutrient-dense – rich in macronutrients (proteins, fats, carbohydrates), micronutrients (vitamins, minerals, dietary fibre) and disease-preventing antioxidants. We can all benefit hugely from incorporating more of these wonderfully nutritious foods into our day.

While it's true that there are some lesser known superfoods – welcome to chia, amaranth and matcha, for example! – it's also easy to find superfoods hiding in plain sight. Just take a look at your fruit bowl – I'm sure it's bursting with amazing, health-supporting foods such as apples and mangoes. And you're probably already packing spinach, cabbage and sweet potato in your vegetable crisper drawer; not forgetting the lentils, oats, nuts and seeds in your pantry. Using these ingredients, and the others outlined in this book, you can enjoy a wide variety of delicious dishes just brimming with nutrients.

While I am not a health professional, rather a passionate foodie with an interest in overall well-being, I would hope that this book will provide inspiration to help you incorporate more of these incredible superfoods into your body to fuel your days. Why supplement when you can go straight to the source? I'd certainly rather eat my vitamins in nutritious, fresh foods than in pill form.

As with my first cookbook, *Greens 24/7*, all of the recipes are vegan, meaning they are free from animal products. My family eats a plant-based diet because of our profound love of animals, but we also love eating this way, especially when there are so many beautiful, nourishing foods that we can cook with instead.

In *Superfoods 24/7* I will show you how to incorporate nutrient-dense superfoods into your day, at every meal, snack, and in-between. Most foods will be familiar to you, but I also hope that you will discover a love for something that you've never tried or never liked before: perhaps it will be a new-found fondness for lentils, an appreciation of the versatility of pumpkin, the subtle sweetness of mineral-rich lucuma or the satiating texture of chia. Whatever it may be, I hope to inspire you to eat, and eat well!

JESS XO

SEEDS AND NUTS

ALMONDS Almonds are so versatile that I can't help but love them. They can be eaten raw, roasted, ground into almond butter, made into milk, baked, used as a salad topper, added to stir-fries . . . the options are endless. They are a wonderful source of vitamin E, important for a strong immune system and skin health, and a good source of plant-based protein, copper, manganese and magnesium to combat stress and promote relaxation.

CHIA SEEDS For such a tiny seed, chia has a huge nutritional profile. They are high in fibre, making them great for digestion and bowel health, and contain calcium and heart-healthy omega-3s. They can absorb ten times their weight in water, which totally transforms their texture, and can help you feel full longer. Available in either black or white varieties and purchased whole or ground, they are on the more expensive end of the superfood spectrum, but a little goes a long way: 1–3 tablespoons per day is plenty.

FLAX SEEDS These little seeds are high in fibre and essential fatty acids; flax is one of the best dietary sources of omega-3 essential fatty acids, has both anti-inflammatory and antioxidant properties, and promotes cardiovascular and colon health. Although I do enjoy the texture of these seeds whole, in order to really benefit from them they are best absorbed if eaten ground or milled. You can buy ground flaxseed, or use a small spice grinder or coffee grinder to pulverise them yourself. Flax is an amazing source of compounds known as lignans, which have been shown to protect against cancer, particularly hormone-related cancers such as breast, uterine and prostate. Flax oil is also available and, like hemp oil, should only be used

HEMP SEEDS Shelled hemp seeds, also known as hemp hearts, have a smooth, nutty flavour and will fill your body with essential fatty acids, specifically heart-healthy omega-3s and omega-6s, in a well-balanced ratio. They are an excellent source of protein, magnesium and fibre, and have also been shown to reduce inflammation and balance hormones. They are an easy and delicious way to make dishes creamy – I sprinkle them on everything! Hemp oil is also available and has the same signature nutty flavour as the hulled seeds; this can be used raw in dressings, sauces, or added to smoothies as a supplement, but should not be used in cooking due to its low smoking point.

BREAKFAST: Pretty-in-pink Strawberry Hemp Smoothie (page 22)

LUNCH: Retro Wedge Salad (page 49)

DINNER: Hemp-crusted Tofu with Garlic-chilli Collards (page 122)

SIDE: Green Beans with Hemp and Almond Breadcrumbs (page 96)

raw in dressings, sauces, or added to smoothies as a supplement. Flax is also my favourite egg substitute in baking cookies and muffins (page 17).

PUMPKIN SEEDS These green seeds, also known as pepitas, are the hulled seeds of a pumpkin. They are tasty little things, rich in iron and magnesium and high in protein: a 30 g (1 oz) serving has more protein than an egg. They're also an excellent source of fibre and the heart-healthy amino acid tryptophan. Add them to trail-mix, granola and cookies as a great source of nut-free protein, making them school-safe too. Opt for raw, unsalted seeds, and if desired you can roast them yourself with a few pinches of sea salt or tamari.

SUNFLOWER SEEDS Sunflower seeds are another winner in the plant-based protein camp. They're also a great source of magnesium, copper, dietary fibre, B vitamins, vitamin E and linoleic acid. They are great by the handful as a snack, and as a topping for soups, salads and cereals. You can also grind them to make your own creamy sunflower seed butter using the method described for almond butter (page 17).

WALNUTS Walnuts are plentiful in omega-3s to support brain and heart health, ellagic acid to support immune function, and are a good source of magnesium, copper and plant-based protein. Although nuts do have a high fat content, multiple studies have shown that regular nut eaters are lower in weight than those who don't regularly consume them.

GRAINS AND PULSES

ADZUKI BEANS These little red beans have been widely used in traditional Japanese sweet and savoury dishes as well as in macrobiotic diets. They are becoming increasingly common now, and I like them because they're rich in protein but don't seem to cause the same gastrointestinal distress that some experience when consuming beans. They have been shown to normalise blood sugar, and are a rich source of fibre – helping to stabilise cholesterol – vitamins and minerals, including vitamin A, folate, phosphorus and magnesium.

AMARANTH Like quinoa, amaranth is a pseudo grain. It's a really small seed that doesn't 'fluff' up as it cooks, similar to polenta. It can also be popped like miniature popcorn! It's a good gluten-free source of protein and fibre, and provides 30 percent of your daily iron needs as well as 12 percent of calcium and a whopping 40 percent of magnesium.

EDAMAME (Shown on page 10) Packed with protein, these little green soyabeans are also a good source of minerals such as calcium, iron, magnesium, phosphorus, potassium, copper, zinc, sodium and manganese, as well as vitamins B6, C, E and folate. They also contain isoflavones, compounds that may be beneficial in managing age-related skin changes in post-menopausal women. Edamame are also plentiful in dietary fibre, which helps maintain a healthy digestive system. You may find fresh edamame at a local farmers' market, but otherwise look in the frozen aisle of the supermarket. As with all soya products, opt for organic where possible.

OATS Oats are so common that you might wonder why they're considered a superfood, but they're a healthy carb choice that can help to lower cholesterol and control blood pressure. They're also high in a starch compound called beta-glucan that helps to stimulate the immune system, and they help you stay fuller for longer so they may be useful in weight control. Look for old-fashioned rolled oats or steel-cut oats – the instant varieties don't have the same health benefits as they've been excessively processed. Pulse oats in your food processor or high-powered blender to make your own oat flour.

QUINOA Although it is often grouped into the category of grains, quinoa is actually a seed so it's referred to as a pseudo cereal or pseudo grain crop. This doesn't make it any less of a superfood, though! Quinoa is a powerhouse of protein and is a very good source of manganese, copper, iron, folate, phosphorus and zinc. Its high magnesium content may help to curb migraine headaches, and it has also been shown to have anti-inflammatory properties. Quinoa is gluten-free and a quick grain to prep – it's great in salads, wellness bowls, porridge and even burger patties.

LENTILS High in fibre, protein and carbohydrates, and low in fat, lentils may be the most nutrient-dense of all pulses. There are several varieties available: green (French) or black (beluga) lentils hold their shape when cooked, while red and yellow lentils become soft and thick. Aside from the fact that they're good for you, they're also super quick to cook and don't require soaking like other dried pulses; I love them in soups, salads, pasta sauces and even in baked goods.

LUNCH: Garlic and Ginger Lentil Soup (page 69)

DINNER: Penne with Lentils, Olives and Kale (page 117)

DESSERT: Double Chocolate Lentil Cookies (page 165)

PARTY FOOD: Curried Lentil-walnut Sliders (page 82)

SPICES AND SEASONINGS

CINNAMON Fragrant cinnamon has been shown to have many health-supporting properties. It contains phytochemicals that can help to combat a yeast overgrowth known as candida, and also has anti-inflammatory compounds that can help to reduce pain from muscle and joint stiffness. In addition it can be used to relieve abdominal pain associated with gas and nausea, and reduce menstrual pain.

GARLIC Although its reputation is for giving us stinky breath, garlic has long been used therapeutically as an expectorant, making it useful in treating asthma, coughs and respiratory issues. It contains phytonutrients that have indicated it may protect against coronary artery disease, infections and cancers, and it is also one of the richest sources of potassium, iron, calcium, magnesium, manganese, zinc and selenium. To benefit from the heart-healthy compound known as allicin, be sure to mince or crush garlic before using it.

GINGER If ever I indulge too much and feel a little sick, I turn to ginger. For me, all it takes is 1 teaspoon of minced ginger steeped in hot water and my tummy is settled. It has a history of being used as an antiseptic, a digestive tonic, and also as an expectorant and remedy for fever as it can promote perspiration. To reap the benefits, it's best used fresh, but even dried ginger can add a punch of flavour to sauces, dressings and baked goods.

TURMERIC We are all familiar with the dried spice common to Indian cooking and curry powders, but turmeric root – a relative of ginger – is often available too; it looks similar to ginger until you slice it open and a brilliant orange-yellow is revealed. Turmeric is believed to help maintain a healthy heart and blood vessels, aid detoxification, and has antiseptic, antibacterial and anti-inflammatory properties. Curcumin, the major active component in turmeric, has been used in the treatment of arthritis and carpal-tunnel syndrome, and studies have also shown it to have antitumour effects. I add it to everything: sweet dishes, savoury dishes, smoothies, and in place of saffron for colouring.

BREAKFAST: Morning Maca Turmeric Smoothie (page 25)

LUNCH: Apple, Beetroot, Broccoli Slaw (page 59)

DINNER: Sunflower Seed, Pineapple and Chickpea Tacos (page 127)

DESSERT: Golden Turmeric Milk (page 171)

ANCIENT SUPERFOODS

ACAI (Shown on page 13) Acai is a berry that originates in the Amazon rainforest. Unless you're local to the Amazon, you're not going to have access to the fresh fruit, but you can find it in frozen purée form (perfect for smoothies), as a juice and as a dried powder. It's a source of potent antioxidants as well as fibre, iron, vitamin A, omega fatty acids and calcium. It is expensive, so it may be more of a treat than an everyday superfood.

GOJI Goji berries are the fruit from a mountainous shrub native to China and Tibet. Perfect for adding to oatmeal, smoothies and cookies, or just for snacking on their own, they're sold dried like raisins, and you'll recognise them for their bright pink hue. High in antioxidants and carotenoids such as beta-carotene, it is believed they may help eyesight. They contain over 18 amino acids, 21 trace minerals, and substantial amounts of vitamins B1, B2, B6, C and E.

LUCUMA Lucuma is a fruit that originates in Peru. After being dried at low temperatures, it's ground to a powder and is used as a mild sweetener. I find its flavour to be a cross between butterscotch and maple syrup. It has a low glycaemic index (GI) rating and is high in beta-carotene and vitamin B3, which contributes to energy production. It has also been shown to contain wound-healing and antiageing properties as well as antimicrobial and antibacterial properties.

MACA Maca powder has been used over the ages for its potent nutritional qualities. It's part of the radish family, and once the roots have been harvested they're dried and ground to a fine powder, which provides calcium, zinc, iron, magnesium and phosphorous, and is rich in vitamins B, C and E. It's also been shown to boost energy and libido while balancing hormones. I find it has a malted caramel flavour, perfect for desserts.

CACAO All true chocolate begins with cacao. Once it is refined and processed, raw cacao becomes cocoa powder, which still retains certain health benefits, but the raw cacao has them all. Most commonly found in powder form and as unsweetened nibs, cacao provides minerals such as magnesium, chromium, iron, zinc, copper and manganese. It's also a concentrated form of fibre and contains potent antioxidants which may help to improve cardiovascular health and strengthen bones. Cacao stimulates the nervous system, improves mood and is even claimed to be a natural aphrodisiac.

BREAKFAST: Walnut Cacao Smoothie (page 24)

DINNER: Cacao Mole Tofu with Slaw (page 126)

DESSERT: Raw Brownie Truffles (page 145)

WINTER WARMER: Superfood Hot Chocolate (page 171)

MATCHA We have all heard that green tea is high in antioxidants, so that would make matcha a super green tea. It is made from the entire green tea leaf, which is ground into a very fine powder, so you are drinking a chlorophyll-rich dose of antioxidants – some suggest it has ten times the benefit of a steeped green tea. It has a slightly grassy flavour and is somewhat of an acquired taste, but once I tried it mixed with steamed almond milk I was hooked. It is both energising and has anti-inflammatory properties too.

FRUITS

APPLE Apples are a great source of fibre and vitamin C, helping to balance blood sugar levels, boost digestion and reduce inflammation. Red-skinned varieties contain anthocyanin antioxidants. Always opt for organic apples where possible.

AVOCADO Beautiful creamy avocados are rich in fibre as well as vitamins A, B6, C, E, K and folate. They may be high in fat, but much of that fat is the heart-healthy kind. They are so versatile, and can be eaten on toast, in a salad, in place of mayo or butter in a sandwich, in raw desserts, and even used to thicken smoothies.

BLUEBERRIES These berries have had a superfood buzz surrounding them for years, and for me they are still the first food that comes to mind when I hear the word 'antioxidant'. Most notably, they have a huge store of proanthocyanidins, which protect against cell degeneration, and are plentiful in vitamin C and fibre.

CITRUS FRUITS There are so many amazing qualities to citrus fruits, just as there are so many delicious varieties. The most common – lemons, limes and oranges – all have a high vitamin C content, which helps the body make use of other vitamins and minerals. Limes are alkalising, and fresh lime or lemon juice with warm water first thing in the morning is an excellent way to start the day and good for liver and kidney function. Lemons have antibacterial properties, aid digestion and are also a mild diuretic. Oranges also have high concentrations of vitamin A, antioxidants, flavonoids, potassium, calcium, magnesium and dietary fibre.

MANGO This tropical fruit is rich in vitamin C and beta-carotene. It contains enzymes that help the body break down protein, so it's great when paired with plant-based proteins such as edamame and hemp seeds. There are two common varieties: large green mangoes, and smaller, sometimes sweeter, yellow-skinned Ataulfo mangoes.

POMEGRANATE (Shown below) Pomegranates are the beautiful pink and red fruits that come into season around the Christmas period. Their juicy seeds (arils) vary from sweet to tangy; I love them and can eat them by the spoonful. Both the juice and the seeds have been shown to have anti-microbial and astringent qualities that both purify and detoxify. They are rich in potassium, phosphorus, sodium, magnesium and calcium as well as vitamins A, B and C.

STRAWBERRIES Strawberries are a rich source of vitamin C and are high in antioxidants and a flavanol compound known as fisetin, which is thought to protect against cancer. They have anti-inflammatory properties and are an excellent source of manganese, which is essential in maintaining bone health. Smaller, sweeter field strawberries are my favourite, but whether from a farm or a grocery store, always opt for organic where possible.

COCONUT Coconuts have something of a bad reputation for being high in fat, however research has shown that they have amazing qualities for both nutritional and health needs. Coconut oil has antibacterial, antifungal and antiviral properties and is a wonderful fat to consume, becoming available to our body as energy almost immediately. The oil is also a good plant source of lauric acid, which helps support a healthy immune system. Coconut milk is energy- and calorie-dense, but it is also rich and creamy and good for curries, desserts and whipped cream. I consider it a wonderful ingredient for occasional use. Coconut meat is high in protein, iron, magnesium, zinc and folate. It's easily found in dried, desiccated or flaked form (opt for unsweetened varieties), or if you're lucky you can source fresh coconuts.

BREAKFAST: Carrot and Sunflower Seed Cookies (page 42)

LUNCH: Coconut Kale Soup with Cashew 'Crème Fraîche' (page 66)

DINNER: Sundried Tomato and Coconut Quinoa Burgers (page 110)

DESSERT: Chai-spiced Coconut Macaroons (page 167)

VEGETABLES

BROCCOLI Like its Brassica family members, broccoli is a good source of vitamins A, C, K and folate, all of which have incredibly important health-promoting roles. It also contains anti-inflammatory, cancer-preventing glucosinolate compounds. And remember: don't throw out those stems – they are delicious and can be peeled and sliced into salads and stir-fry dishes.

BRUSSELS SPROUTS Brussels sprouts may assist in lowering cholesterol and reducing inflammation and are packed with vitamins K, C and folate. As with broccoli, they also contain cancer-preventing glucosinolate compounds. And they look like cute mini cabbage heads – win!

CABBAGE A good source of thiamin, magnesium and phosphorus, as well as dietary fibre, calcium and vitamins B6, C, K and folate, crunchy and refreshing cabbage is not to be missed – and there are so many varieties to choose from.

CARROT As well as the more common orange variety, carrots are also available in purple, red and yellow hues. They are rich in vitamins A, C and K, potassium, dietary fibre and both alpha- and beta-carotene antioxidants, which are needed for eye health and wellness.

KALE Kale is a great source of calcium, vitamin B6, and also has anti-inflammatory properties. With huge amounts of vitamin K (75 g/2½ oz raw kale has almost 700 percent of your daily intake), kale is an incredible source of the vitamin responsible for blood clotting and bone health. It also contains cancer-preventing glucosinolate compounds. Always opt for organic kale where possible.

PUMPKIN Pumpkin contains many health-supporting compounds, such as alpha- and beta-carotenes and zeaxanthin. Carotenes are precursors to vitamin A and support normal growth, immune system function and eye health.

Use pumpkin purée in smoothies, puddings, oatmeal, soups and baking.

SPINACH Spinach is high in calcium, iron, vitamins A, B, E, K and folate – and a rich source of lutein, a carotenoid that supports eye health. Always opt for organic spinach where possible.

SWEET POTATO Vitamin A- and potassium-rich sweet potatoes are so satisfying and very worthy of their superfood status. They contain magnesium for antistress and relaxation benefits; iron; vitamin C, which contributes to collagen production for healthy skin; and vitamin B6, which is thought to help in the prevention of cardiovascular disease. Enjoy them in everything from smoothies to pies!

BREAKFAST: Sweet Potato, Cinnamon and Mango Smoothie (page 26)

DINNER: Chilli-rubbed Sweet Potato Tostadas (page 125)

SIDE: Sweet Potatoes with Walnuts and Pomegranate (page 95)

DESSERT: Sweet Potato 'Cheesecake' (page 168)

THE OTHER INGREDIENTS

You may not be familiar with some of the ingredients used in these recipes, but they're my favourites for good reason. Here's a quick run-down.

BROWN RICE SYRUP This natural sweetener is very thick and sweet like honey or golden syrup, and is perfect for use in granola bars or other recipes that require a sticky binding agent.

COCONUT SUGAR Coconut sugar is an awesome product of the coconut palm tree. The sugar crystals have a similar taste and colour to brown sugar and can be used as a rich-tasting sweetener.

LIQUID AMINOS Also known as Bragg's All Purpose Seasoning, this is another alternative to soya sauce/tamari and is gluten-free.

MEDJOOL DATES (Shown below) These sweet, rich dates are truly nature's caramel. They're perfect for raw desserts, such as the Raw Brownie Truffles (page 145), and also for adding a little extra sweetness to your favourite smoothie. Unless your dates are really soft and tender, they can be soaked in warm water for 10 minutes to soften them up before using as they'll be easier to blend this way.

NUTRITIONAL YEAST Not to be confused with baker's yeast or brewing yeast, nutritional yeast is a flaky powder with a rich 'cheesy' flavour, so it's great for adding to sauces, spreads and even used as a 'breaded' coating. Some brands are fortified with vitamin B12, and these are my first choice.

TAMARI Tamari is my preferred type of soya sauce and hails from the edamame bean. It's a great salty seasoning agent, and gluten-free varieties are available for those who require them.

TOFU Tofu is a great source of plant-based protein made from soyabean curd– also from the edamame bean. It appears in several recipes that showcase its diversity. Many varieties are available, however the two I use most are extra-firm tofu for savoury dishes (found in the refrigerated section of shops), and silken tofu for smooth sauces and desserts (found on the non-perishable shelves of shops). With soya products, it's always best to choose organic, if available.

UMEBOSHI VINEGAR Also known as ume plum vinegar, this is the brine left over after pickling Japanese ume plums with shiso leaf. It's something I reach for often when making dressings and sauces as it has a really strong, salty flavour with tons of bite: a little goes a long way.

UNREFINED CANE SUGAR Also known as evaporated cane juice or organic cane sugar, this is my choice for a granulated, vegan sweetener. It still contains molasses so has a good depth of flavour.

BASIC SKILLS

Throughout the book, some ingredients are used regularly in the recipes. Below are a few basic tricks-of-the-trade to help you prepare these ingredients for cooking.

KALE To strip kale from its stem, separate as many stalks of kale from the bunch as you need, keeping the woody stem intact. Grip the base of one stalk in one hand. With the other hand, form a loose 'claw' and run your hand from the base of the stalk along the stem, stripping the leaf free as you go. Discard the stems and you're left with the leaves. Slice or chop as needed.

FLAX EGG To make one flax egg, mix 1 tablespoon of ground flaxseed with 3 tablespoons of water and leave for 5 minutes. The mixture will gel and become a bit gloopy, like a raw egg. Stir again and the 'egg' is ready for use in baked goods such as muffins, pancakes and quick breads. It's not so good as a direct replacement for eggs in crème brûlée or omelettes.

CHIA EGG To make one chia egg, mix 1 tablespoon of whole or ground chia seeds with 3 tablespoons of water and leave for 5 minutes. The mixture will gel and become a bit gloopy, like a raw egg. Stir again and the 'egg' is ready for use. As above, it's best used in baked goods.

ALMOND BUTTER To make almond butter, place 170–340 g (5¾–12 oz) of almonds (raw or roasted) in a food processor and grind until butter is formed. This can take between 10 and 15 minutes; after 3 to 4 minutes you'll have finely ground nuts, then the oils will begin to release, the mixture will begin to heat and slowly it will turn into butter. Stop to scrape down the sides every couple minutes to ensure all the nuts are incorporated and also to prevent your processor from overheating. Once it's silky smooth, you can add flavourings, if desired – a pinch of sea salt or a little vanilla and cinnamon work well. Store in a glass jar in the fridge for up to two weeks.

ALMOND MILK To make almond milk, you'll need to soak the nuts for 8 hours in water, then drain and rinse. Place 170 g (5¾ oz) of soaked nuts in a blender with 1 litre (35 fl oz) of water. Blend on high for 1 to 2 minutes. Strain the liquid through a nut milk bag (a fine nylon mesh bag) into a bowl; if you don't have one, use a fine mesh sieve lined with cheesecloth. Squeeze the bag to get every last bit of goodness out of it. Transfer to a glass container and store in the fridge for up to five days. The milk will separate – just give it a good stir before enjoying.

PUMPKIN PURÉE For pumpkin purée, wash and dry one or two small pumpkins or pie pumpkins, then slice off their tops. Cut each in half and scoop out the seeds and stringy guts (save the seeds for roasting for a crunchy snack). Cut each half in half again and place on a baking sheet. Bake at 175°C (350°F) for 45 minutes, or until the flesh is tender and easily pierced by a fork. Remove from the oven and leave until cool to the touch. Peel off the skins and purée the flesh in a food processor until smooth. If the purée seems thin, strain it through a nut milk bag or cheesecloth set over a bowl. Discard the liquid and the purée is ready for use in your favourite recipe.

'TYPICAL DAY' SUPERFOOD MEAL PLANS

Wondering how to put it all together? Here are a few sample meal plans showing you how to eat your superfoods throughout the day.

FOR THE PARENT TRYING TO FEED THEIR KIDS SUPERFOODS

BREAKFAST: Fluffy Banana Chia Pancakes (page 35)

LUNCH: Black Bean Hemp Patties (page 109)

SNACK: Baked Almond Granola Bars (page 159)

DINNER: Sweet Potato Mac 'n' Cheese (page 113)

DESSERT: Adzuki Bean Brownies (page 148)

FOR THE SUPER-BUSY, NO-TIME-TO-SLAVE-OVER-A-MEAL COOK

BREAKFAST: Energising Matcha Kale Smoothie (page 25)

LUNCH: Amaranth with Turmeric, Cranberry and Almonds (page 90)

SNACK: No-bake Quinoa Cereal Bars (page 157)

DINNER: Vegetable Quinoa 'Fried Rice' (page 137)

DESSERT: Three-ingredient Chia Pudding (page 150)

FOR THE HEALTH-CONSCIOUS TRYING TO MAXIMISE NUTRITIOUS CONTENT

BREAKFAST: Morning Maca Turmeric Smoothie (page 25)

LUNCH: Avocado-massaged Kale Salad (page 55)

SNACK: Morning Glory Muffins (page 154)

DINNER: Tempeh Brassica Bibimbap (page 106)

DESSERT: Goji Almond Energy Bites (page 147)

FOR THOSE WHO LOVE TO ENTERTAIN

BREAKFAST: Buckwheat Maca Waffles with Pomegranate Syrup (page 40)

LUNCH: Spinach and Pomegranate Salad (page 50)

SNACK: Sunflower Seed Pâté (page 81)

DINNER: Penne with Lentils, Olives and Kale (page 117)

DESSERT: Sweet Potato 'Cheesecake' (page 168)

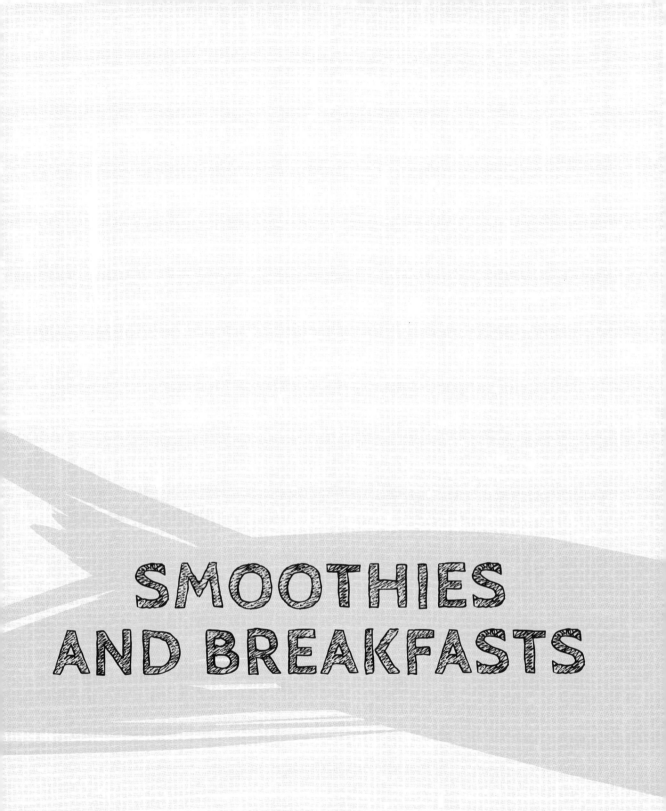

SMOOTHIES
AND BREAKFASTS

PRETTY-IN-PINK STRAWBERRY HEMP SMOOTHIE

Serves 2
gluten-free

Perky, sweet strawberries are mellowed out with creamy, slightly nutty hemp seeds. This smoothie boasts around 20% iron and 100% vitamin C per serving.

Prep: 5 mins

300 g (10½ oz) chopped strawberries

35 g (1¼ oz) shelled hemp seeds, plus 1 teaspoon for sprinkling

225 g (8 oz) frozen peach chunks

250 ml (9 fl oz) water or non-dairy milk (of choice)

1 Place all the ingredients in a blender and blend on high until smooth and frothy. A little more liquid can be added if needed for a thinner blend. Pour into glasses and serve immediately.

SUPERFOOD TIP: Play with flavours by using different non-dairy milks or coconut water in smoothies.

CALORIES (PER SERVING)	201
PROTEIN	9.1 G
TOTAL FAT	9.7 G
SATURATED FAT	0.9 G
CARBOHYDRATES	23.5 G
DIETARY FIBRE	5.3 G
SUGARS	16.8 G
VITAMINS	C

CITRUS CHIA POM SMOOTHIE

Serves 1
gluten-free

The name of this smoothie speaks for itself — it's a superfood flavour explosion with plenty of potassium, vitamin C and antioxidants.

Prep: 5 mins

75 g (2½ oz) pomegranate arils (see tip, page 40)

250 ml (9 fl oz) orange juice

1–2 tablespoons chia seeds

1 frozen banana

1 Place all the ingredients in a blender and blend on high until smooth and frothy. Pour into a glass and serve immediately.

VARIATION: If pomegranates aren't available, reduce orange juice to 190 ml (6½ fl oz) and add 60 ml (2 fl oz) of pomegranate juice and 30 g (1 oz) of raspberries.

CALORIES (PER SERVING)	306
PROTEIN	5.1 G
TOTAL FAT	3.4 G
SATURATED FAT	0 G
CARBOHYDRATES	70.1 G
DIETARY FIBRE	6.6 G
SUGARS	42.8 G
VITAMINS	B6, C

BLISSFUL BLUEBERRY OATMEAL SMOOTHIE

Serves 2
gluten-free
option

Oats blend up nicely in this smoothie, and add fibre and extra superfood sustenance to keep you going all morning. For a gluten-free option, use gluten-free oats.

Prep: 5 mins

215 g (7½ oz) frozen blueberries
125 ml (4½ fl oz) non-dairy vanilla yogurt
25 g (¾ oz) rolled oats
500 ml (18 fl oz) almond milk (page 17)
2–4 ice cubes (optional)

1 Place all the ingredients in a blender and blend on high until smooth and frothy. Add a few ice cubes to make it even frothier, if desired. Pour into glasses and serve immediately.

CALORIES (PER SERVING)	199
PROTEIN	3.9 G
TOTAL FAT	5.0 G
SATURATED FAT	0 G
CARBOHYDRATES	37.2 G
DIETARY FIBRE	6.1 G
SUGARS	17.1 G
VITAMINS	B6, C, E

WALNUT CACAO SMOOTHIE

Serves 2
gluten-free

A sweet, nutty start to the day, made all the better by the omega-3s from the walnuts that support brain health, and the free-radical-fighting antioxidants in the cacao.

Prep: 5 mins

25 g (¾ oz) chopped walnuts
250 ml (9 fl oz) water
1 frozen banana
2 pitted medjool dates, chopped
2 teaspoons cacao powder
1 tablespoon almond butter (page 17)
2–3 ice cubes
1 teaspoon cacao nibs, to serve

1 Place the walnuts, water, banana and dates in a blender and blend on high until smooth.

2 Add the cacao powder, almond butter and ice cubes and blend again to combine. Pour into a glass, top with cacao nibs, and serve.

VARIATION: For a caffeinated option, add one shot of espresso before blending.

CALORIES (PER SERVING)	241
PROTEIN	5.4 G
TOTAL FAT	13.7 G
SATURATED FAT	1.8 G
CARBOHYDRATES	29.5 G
DIETARY FIBRE	5.2 G
SUGARS	16.6 G
VITAMINS	B6, E

MORNING MACA TURMERIC SMOOTHIE

Serves 2
gluten-free

Turmeric shines (literally!) in this smoothie, with its healing, anti-inflammatory qualities. This is so thick and delicious that it can be enjoyed with a spoon.

Prep: 5 mins

280 g (10 oz) frozen papaya chunks
1 extra-ripe banana
250 ml (9 fl oz) coconut water
2 teaspoons maca powder
½–1 teaspoon turmeric
2 tablespoons goji berries, to serve

1 Place the papaya, banana and coconut water in a blender and blend on high until smooth and creamy.

2 Add the maca and turmeric and blend again to combine. A little more liquid can be added if needed for a smoother blend or if you prefer a thinner smoothie. Pour into glasses, top with goji berries, and serve.

CALORIES (PER SERVING)	209
PROTEIN	2.3 G
TOTAL FAT	1.5 G
SATURATED FAT	0 G
CARBOHYDRATES	50.1 G
DIETARY FIBRE	6.2 G
SUGARS	36.1 G
VITAMINS	A, C

ENERGISING MATCHA KALE SMOOTHIE

Serves 2
gluten-free

Forget morning coffee – this smoothie will give you all the perk you need. Aside from matcha's antioxidant superpowers, it comes with a hefty side of calcium, too.

Prep: 5 mins

2 frozen bananas
75 g (2½ oz) kale leaves
375 ml (13 fl oz) almond milk (page 17)
3–4 ice cubes
1 rounded teaspoon matcha powder

1 Place the banana, kale, almond milk and ice cubes in a blender and blend on high until smooth.

2 Add the matcha powder and blend again to combine. Pour into glasses and serve immediately.

CALORIES (PER SERVING)	155
PROTEIN	6.1 G
TOTAL FAT	2.4 G
SATURATED FAT	0 G
CARBOHYDRATES	31.4 G
DIETARY FIBRE	7.4 G
SUGARS	14.4 G
VITAMINS	A, B6, C, E

SWEET POTATO, CINNAMON AND MANGO SMOOTHIE

Use up any leftover baked sweet potatoes in this glorious golden smoothie.

Prep: 5 mins

150 g (5 oz) frozen mango chunks
100 g (3½ oz) chopped cooked sweet potato
1 teaspoon cinnamon
125 ml (4½ fl oz) pineapple juice
190 ml (6½ fl oz) water
½ teaspoon vanilla extract
1 teaspoon agave nectar (optional)

1 Place all the ingredients in a blender and blend on high until smooth and creamy. Pour into glasses and serve immediately.

SUPERFOOD TIP: Bake a few extra sweet potatoes to keep in the fridge, so you're ready to go whenever you fancy a smoothie!

CALORIES (PER SERVING)	136
PROTEIN	1.7 G
TOTAL FAT	0.4 G
SATURATED FAT	0 G
CARBOHYDRATES	32.5 G
DIETARY FIBRE	3.8 G
SUGARS	21.1 G
VITAMINS	A, B6, C

SPICED PUMPKIN POWER SMOOTHIE

This smoothie screams autumn, but can be enjoyed any time using tinned pumpkin.

Prep: 5 mins

1 frozen banana
220 g (7¾ oz) pumpkin purée (page 17) or tinned pumpkin
375 ml (13 fl oz) soya milk
2 pitted medjool dates
½ tablespoon black treacle
1 teaspoon minced fresh ginger
½ teaspoon cinnamon
¼ teaspoon nutmeg
pinch of ground cloves

1 Place all the ingredients in a blender and blend on high until smooth and creamy. Pour into glasses and serve immediately.

SUPERFOOD TIP: Increase the sweetness of a smoothie by adding 1 tablespoon of lucuma powder, maple syrup, agave nectar or pitted medjool dates (as here).

CALORIES (PER SERVING)	265
PROTEIN	8.5 G
TOTAL FAT	4.3 G
SATURATED FAT	0.6 G
CARBOHYDRATES	50.5 G
DIETARY FIBRE	7.0 G
SUGARS	30.5 G
VITAMINS	A

KALE AND PEAR SMOOTHIE

Serves 1
gluten-free

Why not start your day with a glass of iron- and calcium-rich kale? The secret to this smoothie's creaminess is the avocado, which comes with an extra dose of healthy fats.

Prep: 5 mins

1 ripe pear, peeled and cored
75 g (2½ oz) kale, woody stems removed (page 17)
1 frozen banana
¼ avocado
375 ml (13 fl oz) vanilla almond milk

1 Place all the ingredients in a blender and blend on high until smooth and creamy. Pour into a glass and serve immediately.

SUPERFOOD TIP: Adding avocado to a smoothie creates a thick, whipped texture.

CALORIES (PER SERVING)	326
PROTEIN	5.9 G
TOTAL FAT	9.4 G
SATURATED FAT	1.2 G
CARBOHYDRATES	62.3 G
DIETARY FIBRE	10.1 G
SUGARS	28.1 G
VITAMINS	A, B6, C

LUCUMA ALMOND-BUTTER SHAKE

A decadently rich smoothie. Lucuma powder comes from the dried Peruvian fruit, and as well as adding a maple flavour, it contains iron, beta-carotene and zinc.

Prep: 5 mins

2 frozen bananas
375 ml (13 fl oz) almond milk (page 17)
60 g (2 oz) smooth almond butter (page 17)
2 tablespoons lucuma powder
2–4 ice cubes

1 Place all the ingredients in a blender and blend on high until smooth and frothy. Pour into glasses and serve immediately.

SUPERFOOD TIP: Using frozen bananas makes a thicker, creamier smoothie.

CALORIES (PER SERVING)	373
PROTEIN	8.9 G
TOTAL FAT	18.9 G
SATURATED FAT	2.6 G
CARBOHYDRATES	47.5 G
DIETARY FIBRE	6.8 G
SUGARS	19.3 G
VITAMINS	C, E

FRESH BERRY CHIA JAM

It will be hard to justify using shop-bought jam once you realise you can have the fresh, homemade variety in 30 minutes. Use whatever fresh berries you like!

Prep: 5 mins | Cook: 10 mins (plus 20 mins' setting time)

120–150 g (4¼–5 oz) berries of choice (strawberry, raspberry, blueberry, blackberry)
1 tablespoon water
2 tablespoons maple syrup (or to taste, depending on the ripeness of the fruit)
1 teaspoon lemon juice
2 tablespoons chia seeds

See image, page 31

1 Place the berries and water in a small saucepan over a medium heat for 5 to 7 minutes until soft. Mash the fruit, leaving a few bigger pieces. Stir in the maple syrup and lemon juice.

2 Remove from the heat, stir in the chia seeds, and continue to stir for 2 to 3 minutes. Leave for another 20 minutes, then stir again. If the jam is too thin for your liking, it will continue to thicken as it sits; or place it in the fridge to speed up the process. Any leftover jam can be stored in a jar in the fridge for up to one week.

CALORIES (PER 1 CUP/340 G)	212
PROTEIN	4.0 G
TOTAL FAT	5.6 G
SATURATED FAT	0 G
CARBOHYDRATES	44.5 G
DIETARY FIBRE	8.0 G
SUGARS	31.3 G
VITAMINS	C

ORANGE CACAO-CHIP BREAKFAST BISCUITS

Makes 10

Cacao nibs are not sweet like chocolate chips, but their numerous health benefits
— mood-enhancing chemicals, mega magnesium stores and iron — make up for it.
Lighter than a traditional biscuit, these are perfect for any special breakfast occasion,
especially served with the Fresh Berry Chia Jam (page 29).

Prep: 15 mins | Cook: 15 mins

100 g (3½ oz) plain flour
100 g (3½ oz) whole-wheat flour
1½ teaspoons baking powder
½ teaspoon bicarbonate of soda
¼ teaspoon sea salt
1 teaspoon cinnamon
150 g (5 oz) brown sugar
110 g (4 oz) pure vegetable shortening
1 flax egg (page 17)
60 ml (2 fl oz) almond milk (page 17)
2 tablespoons orange juice
1 tablespoon orange zest
40 g (1½ oz) cacao nibs

1 Preheat the oven to 200°C (400°F). In a large bowl, mix together the flours, baking powder, bicarbonate of soda, sea salt, cinnamon and sugar. Cube the shortening and cut it into the flour mixture using two forks or a pastry cutter.

2 Add the flax egg and mix lightly, followed by the milk, orange juice and zest. Mix until the dry ingredients are just incorporated, then gently fold in the cacao nibs.

3 The dough will be very sticky, but if it's too sticky to work with, add another tablespoon or two of flour. With floured hands, scoop up about 60 g (2 oz) at a time and pat it into a round as you transfer it to a lined baking sheet. Leave 5 cm (2 inches) between each one as they will spread out as they bake. Bake for 12 to 15 minutes, then remove from the oven and leave to cool.

CALORIES (PER SERVING)	266
PROTEIN	2.9 G
TOTAL FAT	13.6 G
SATURATED FAT	5.7 G
CARBOHYDRATES	33.2 G
DIETARY FIBRE	2.6 G
SUGARS	15.1 G
VITAMINS	C

ACAI SMOOTHIE BOWL WITH SUPERFOOD TOPPINGS

Serves 1
gluten-free

This smoothie is full of the Brazilian superfood acai and comes with heaps of antioxidants as well as vitamin A, iron and some heart-healthy omega fats, too. Plus the beautiful purple smoothie bowl provides a blank canvas for all the superfood toppings your heart desires.

Prep: 5 mins

1 x 100 g (3½ oz) packet frozen acai purée

1 banana

165 g (5½ oz) pineapple chunks

60 ml (2 fl oz) water or non-dairy milk (of choice)

1 tablespoon protein powder (of choice) (e.g. hemp, pea or brown rice)

SUGGESTED TOPPINGS

granola; desiccated coconut; cacao nibs; slivered almonds; shelled hemp seeds; chia seeds; fresh berries; almond butter

1 Place all the ingredients in a blender and blend on high until smooth and creamy. A little more liquid can be added if needed for a smoother blend, but keep in mind that it is intended to be thick enough to eat with a spoon.

2 Pour into a bowl, add your choice of toppings, and enjoy.

VARIATION: If acai purée isn't available, use frozen blueberries instead.

CALORIES (PER SERVING)	237
PROTEIN	7.5 G
TOTAL FAT	3.6 G
SATURATED FAT	0 G
CARBOHYDRATES	50.9 G
DIETARY FIBRE	10.0 G
SUGARS	31.0 G
VITAMINS	B6, C

BLUEBERRY CHIA OVERNIGHT OATS

Serves 2
gluten-free
option

This is one of my favourite summer breakfasts, perfect for a filling, wholesome start to the day. All it takes is a few minutes' preparation the night before, and then the magic happens while you sleep. For a gluten-free option, use gluten-free oats.

**Prep: 5 mins
(plus 1–8 hours' soaking)**

60 g (2 oz) rolled oats (not quick-cook)

2 tablespoons chia seeds

2 teaspoons maca powder

375–500 ml (13–18 fl oz) unsweetened almond milk (page 17)

1–2 teaspoons agave nectar or maple syrup

75 g (2½ oz) fresh blueberries

¼ teaspoon cinnamon

2 tablespoons chopped almonds (optional)

2 tablespoons Fresh Berry Chia Jam (page 29) (optional)

See image, page 32, rear

1 Mix the oats, chia seeds and maca powder together in a bowl. Pour in the almond milk, stir, and set aside in the fridge for at least an hour, or ideally overnight.

2 When you're ready to eat, add a little agave or maple syrup to taste, fold in the blueberries and sprinkle with cinnamon. For a little extra crunch (and protein), add chopped almonds, or for extra sweetness serve with the chia jam.

VARIATIONS: To enjoy this breakfast warm: follow step 1 above, then heat the oat and milk mixture in a saucepan for about 10 to 15 minutes until heated through. Sweeten with agave or maple syrup, fold in the berries and cinnamon and enjoy.

If you can't get hold of fresh blueberries, use frozen berries instead. Fold the frozen berries into the oat and milk mixture the night before and they will thaw in the fridge overnight. If making the warm version of the dish, cook the frozen berries in the oats for 3 to 5 minutes, or until they are warmed through.

CALORIES (PER SERVING)	216
PROTEIN	7.1 G
TOTAL FAT	7.2 G
SATURATED FAT	0.5 G
CARBOHYDRATES	35.9 G
DIETARY FIBRE	8.2 G
SUGARS	7.7 G
VITAMINS	B6, E

FLUFFY BANANA CHIA PANCAKES

Serves 4 gluten-free option

These fluffy pancakes make weekends extra special. Chia seeds work their magic, creating little pancake pillows and providing fibre-rich carbohydrates and calcium. For a gluten-free option, use an equal mix of oat and gluten-free blend flours.

Prep: 5 mins | Cook: 20 mins

250 g (9 oz) whole-wheat flour
4 teaspoons baking powder
2 teaspoons bicarbonate of soda
pinch of salt
2 bananas
2 tablespoons chia seeds
500 ml (18 fl oz) almond milk
(page 17)

See image, page 20, rear

1 In a large bowl, combine the flour, baking powder, bicarbonate of soda and salt.

2 In another bowl, mash the bananas until smooth. Add the chia seeds and milk and stir well.

3 Add the wet ingredients to the dry ingredients and whisk until no lumps remain.

4 Preheat a frying pan. Using 60 ml (2 fl oz) of batter for each pancake, cook for 4 to 5 minutes on each side, until lightly browned and no longer doughy.

VARIATION: Take these pancakes to the next level by adding an extra flavour to the batter in step 3. Try one of the following options: 2 tablespoons cacao nibs or chocolate chips; 85 g (3 oz) pineapple chunks; 1 teaspoon cinnamon; 30 g (1 oz) desiccated coconut; 75 g (2½ oz) blueberries.

CALORIES (PER SERVING)	315
PROTEIN	8.4 G
TOTAL FAT	3.4 G
SATURATED FAT	0 G
CARBOHYDRATES	65.5 G
DIETARY FIBRE	5.1 G
SUGARS	7.4 G
VITAMINS	A, E

PUMPKIN BAKED OATMEAL

A bowl of oatmeal might not be fancy enough for guests, but this baked oatmeal dish certainly is. It's a breeze to put together and the best part is that while it's cooking, your kitchen will smell delicious. For a gluten-free option, use gluten-free oats.

Prep: 10 mins | Cook: 25 mins

220 g (7¾ oz) pumpkin purée (page 17) or tinned pumpkin

375 ml (13 fl oz) almond milk, plus extra to serve (page 17)

2 tablespoons maple syrup

½ tablespoon black treacle

1½ teaspoons cinnamon

1 teaspoon nutmeg

⅛ teaspoon sea salt

2 tablespoons melted coconut oil, plus extra for greasing

225 g (8 oz) rolled oats

65 g (2¼ oz) pecans, toasted

1 Preheat the oven to 190°C (375°F). In a large bowl, mix together the pumpkin, almond milk, maple syrup, black treacle, spices and salt.

2 Add 2 tablespoons of coconut oil and the oats and stir until just combined. Fold in the toasted pecans.

3 Spread the batter into a greased 23 x 33-cm (9 x 13-inch) baking dish. Flatten the mixture out to the edges and bake for 20 to 25 minutes, or until lightly browned around the edges and on top. Remove from the oven and serve warm, with a splash of almond milk, if desired. Any leftovers will continue to 'set', and you'll then be able to slice it into oatmeal bars for breakfasts on the run (see image opposite).

CALORIES (PER SERVING)	215
PROTEIN	5.0 G
TOTAL FAT	11.7 G
SATURATED FAT	3.9 G
CARBOHYDRATES	23.9 G
DIETARY FIBRE	4.8 G
SUGARS	2.2 G
VITAMINS	A

QUINOA PORRIDGE WITH BROWNIE CRUMBLES

Serves 4
gluten-free

Sometimes it's a real treat to have something as indulgent as chocolate for breakfast. Yet this dish is still full of goodness thanks to quinoa, anti-ageing lucuma, hormone-balancing maca and powerful cacao-rich Raw Brownie Truffles (page 145) on top.

Prep: 5 mins | Cook: 20 mins

170 g (5¾ oz) quinoa
625 ml (21 fl oz) almond milk (page 17) or other non-dairy milk (of choice)
2 tablespoons lucuma powder
2 teaspoons maca powder
2 Raw Brownie Truffles, crumbled (page 145)

1 Bring the quinoa and almond milk to a boil in a small saucepan over a medium heat. Cover, reduce heat to low, and simmer for around 15 minutes, or until the quinoa is tender and a thick porridge remains.

2 Remove from the heat and stir in the lucuma and maca powders. Cover and leave to rest for 5 minutes, then fluff with a fork. Divide the porridge between bowls and serve topped with brownie crumbles.

VARIATION: Add a burst of colour and even more antioxidants by adding fresh berries or 2 tablespoons of goji berries.

CALORIES (PER SERVING) (PORRIDGE ONLY)	210
PROTEIN	7.3 G
TOTAL FAT	4.2 G
SATURATED FAT	0 G
CARBOHYDRATES	35.1 G
DIETARY FIBRE	3.8 G
SUGARS	1.2 G
VITAMINS	B6, B12, E

BUCKWHEAT MACA WAFFLES WITH POMEGRANATE SYRUP

Serves 4

Wholesome buckwheat waffles get a boost of power and vitality from cinnamon and maca, while the delectable pomegranate-infused maple syrup puts this brunch in a class of its own.

Prep: 20 mins | Cook: 15 mins

125 g (4½ oz) buckwheat flour
125 g (4½ oz) plain flour
2 tablespoons maca powder
2 teaspoons cinnamon
1 tablespoon baking powder
½ teaspoon sea salt
500 ml (18 fl oz) non-dairy milk (of choice)
3 tablespoons coconut oil
2 tablespoons maple syrup
40 g (1½ oz) pomegranate arils, to serve

FOR THE POMEGRANATE SYRUP
60 ml (2 fl oz) pomegranate juice
¼ tablespoon maple syrup

See image, page 20, front

1 Preheat a waffle-maker, if you have one. If not, you can use a griddle pan, as directed in step 4.

2 In a large bowl, combine the dry ingredients. Stir in the milk, oil and maple syrup until a smooth batter forms, being careful not to overwork it. Set it aside to rest for 10 minutes.

3 Meanwhile, for the pomegranate syrup, put the pomegranate juice and the maple syrup in a small saucepan over a medium heat. Cook, stirring occasionally, for 10 to 15 minutes, or until the syrup has reduced and thickened slightly.

4 Cook the batter according to your specific waffle-maker instructions. If you don't have a waffle-maker, heat a griddle pan over a medium heat until hot. Brush with oil and add 125 ml (4½ fl oz) of batter to the pan for each waffle. Allow to cook for 3 to 4 minutes, then flip and cook for another 3 to 4 minutes, until golden. The waffles can be placed in a single layer on a cooling rack and kept warm in a 200°C (400°F) oven while the rest of the batch is prepared. Serve the waffles hot, topped with the pomegranate syrup and arils.

SUPERFOOD TIP: To open and seed a pomegranate, score around the equator with a sharp knife (don't cut through the pith). Pry the halves apart. Working over a bowl, cup one of the halves in your palm, seed-side down, and using a wooden spoon, hit the back of it several times, while using your fingers to spin the fruit around in your palm. The seeds, also known as arils, will fall out into the bowl.

CALORIES (PER SERVING)	488
PROTEIN	12 G
TOTAL FAT	13.8 G
SATURATED FAT	9.4 G
CARBOHYDRATES	82.9 G
DIETARY FIBRE	6 G
SUGARS	27.4 G
VITAMINS	C

COCONUT MILK AMARANTH RICE PUDDING

Serves 4
gluten-free

This is a cross between traditional rice pudding and coconut sticky rice with mango. It's sweet, it's filling, it's packed with superfoods, and it's especially quick to make if you already have leftover rice in the fridge.

Prep: 5 mins | Cook: 40 mins

50 g (1¾ oz) amaranth

380 g (13½ oz) cooked brown rice

500 ml (18 fl oz) drinkable coconut milk or 1 x 400 g (14 oz) tin light coconut milk

2 tablespoons water

¼ teaspoon orange zest

2 tablespoons maple syrup

pinch of cardamom, plus extra to serve

60 g (2 oz) raisins (optional)

1 ripe mango, peeled and cubed

See image, page 43, rear

1 In a large pot, bring the amaranth, rice, coconut milk, water, orange zest and maple syrup to a rapid simmer over a medium heat. Reduce the heat to low and simmer gently for 15 to 20 minutes, stirring every few minutes to prevent the amaranth from sticking to the sides and bottom of the pot.

2 Once the liquid has been absorbed and the pudding is thick, stir in the cardamom and raisins, if using.

3 Remove from the heat and leave to cool for 5 to 10 minutes, then serve into bowls and top with cubes of mango and a pinch of cardamom.

VARIATIONS: If cardamom is unavailable, use cinnamon instead.

This breakfast can also be served chilled. The pudding may become slightly gelatinous as it sits, so prior to serving give it a good stir and add a splash of non-dairy milk of your choice if necessary.

CALORIES (PER SERVING)	312
PROTEIN	4.6 G
TOTAL FAT	8.8 G
SATURATED FAT	6.5 G
CARBOHYDRATES	53.2 G
DIETARY FIBRE	2.8 G
SUGARS	17.8 G
VITAMINS	C

CARROT AND SUNFLOWER SEED COOKIES

Makes 12

A wholesome, nutrient-rich breakfast cookie is great to have on hand when you've got a busy morning. It makes breakfasts on the run — and midday snacking — easy, while still packing a superfood punch.

Prep: 15 mins | Cook: 20 mins

125 g (4½ oz) whole-wheat flour
½ teaspoon baking powder
¼ teaspoon fine sea salt
1 teaspoon cinnamon
½ teaspoon nutmeg
85 g (3 oz) almond butter (page 17)
125 g (4½ oz) unsweetened apple sauce
25 g (¾ oz) ground flax meal
60 ml (2 fl oz) melted coconut oil
4 tablespoons maple syrup
1 teaspoon minced fresh ginger
110 g (4 oz) grated carrot
75 g (2½ oz) shelled sunflower seeds

1 Preheat the oven to 160°C (325°F). In a large bowl, combine the flour, baking powder, salt, cinnamon and nutmeg.

2 In another bowl, mix together the almond butter, apple sauce, flax meal, coconut oil, maple syrup and ginger.

3 Add the wet ingredients to the dry ingredients along with the carrots and sunflower seeds, and mix to incorporate.

4 Drop giant spoonfuls onto a lined baking sheet and flatten gently with the back of the spoon; they won't spread during baking. Bake for 18 to 22 minutes, or until the cookies no longer appear 'wet'. Allow to cool for 5 minutes on the baking sheet before removing to a cooling rack.

CALORIES (PER SERVING)	191
PROTEIN	4.3 G
TOTAL FAT	12.3 G
SATURATED FAT	4.6 G
CARBOHYDRATES	17.9 G
DIETARY FIBRE	2.2 G
SUGARS	5.7 G
VITAMINS	A

SALADS AND SOUPS

KICK-START QUINOA SALAD

Let this lunchtime salad kick-start your energy supplies and help you get through the rest of your day. Quinoa contains 50% more protein than wheat and cooks in just 15 minutes – perfect for quick, nutritious meals.

Prep: 10 mins | Cook: 25 mins

170 g (5¾ oz) quinoa

440 ml (15 fl oz) water

150 g (5 oz) halved grape tomatoes

100 g (3½ oz) seeded and diced cucumber

75 g (2½ oz) shelled edamame beans, blanched

5 g (⅛ oz) basil, chopped

1 spring onion, diced

2 tablespoons extra-virgin olive oil

2 tablespoons fresh lime juice

sea salt and freshly ground black pepper, to taste

1 Rinse the quinoa well in a fine mesh sieve. In a small saucepan, bring the quinoa and water to a boil, then reduce the heat to a low simmer, cover, and cook for 15 minutes or until all the liquid has been absorbed. Remove from the heat and leave, covered, for an additional 5 minutes. Fluff with a fork and transfer to a large bowl to cool for 10 minutes.

2 Fold in the tomatoes, cucumber, edamame, basil and onion.

3 In a small bowl, whisk together the olive oil, lime juice and ¼ teaspoon of salt. Pour over the quinoa and toss to combine. Season to taste and serve.

CALORIES (PER SERVING)	259
PROTEIN	9.1 G
TOTAL FAT	11 G
SATURATED FAT	1.5 G
CARBOHYDRATES	33 G
DIETARY FIBRE	4.5 G
SUGARS	1.7 G
VITAMINS	B6, C

RETRO WEDGE SALAD

Serves 4
gluten-free

Here's a superfood spin on this popular salad of days gone by. The hemp- and nut-based dressing is every bit as yummy, and full of protein and fibre.

Prep: 10 mins | Cook: 5 mins

1 head Boston or iceberg lettuce, quartered

75 g (2½ oz) halved grape or cherry tomatoes

½ avocado, cubed

1 tablespoon chopped chives

FOR THE HEMP DRESSING

75 g (2½ oz) shelled hemp seeds

40 g (1½ oz) raw cashews, soaked for 4 to 6 hours

1 tablespoon lemon juice

2 tablespoons umeboshi vinegar

60 ml (2 fl oz) water

1 For the dressing, place all the ingredients in a food processor and blend until smooth. More water can be added, ½ tablespoon at a time, until a thick, pourable dressing is achieved.

2 Place each quarter of lettuce on a plate with a few tomatoes and pieces of chopped avocado. Top with the hemp dressing and sprinkle with the chives.

CALORIES (PER SERVING)	239
PROTEIN	8.9 G
TOTAL FAT	18.5 G
SATURATED FAT	2.8 G
CARBOHYDRATES	12.4 G
DIETARY FIBRE	3.8 G
SUGARS	2.3 G
VITAMINS	B6

ROCKET AND BERRY SALAD

Serves 4
gluten-free

This summery salad is brimming with vitamin- and antioxidant-rich berries and omega power from the flax oil dressing.

Prep: 5 mins

120 g (4¼ oz) rocket

½ sweet, mild onion, thinly sliced

150 g (5 oz) sliced strawberries

75 g (2½ oz) fresh blueberries

75 g (2½ oz) fresh blackberries

FOR THE VINAIGRETTE

3 tablespoons flax oil

2 tablespoons red wine vinegar

1 garlic clove, minced

sea salt and freshly ground black pepper, to taste

See image, page 44

1 Place the rocket, onion and half the berries in a large salad bowl.

2 For the dressing, combine the flax oil, vinegar, garlic and seasoning, add to the salad and toss. Top with the remaining berries and serve.

CALORIES (PER SERVING)	108
PROTEIN	1.3 G
TOTAL FAT	8.8 G
SATURATED FAT	0.6 G
CARBOHYDRATES	7.8 G
DIETARY FIBRE	2.3 G
SUGARS	4.5 G
VITAMINS	A, B6, C

SPINACH AND POMEGRANATE SALAD

Serves 4
gluten-free

This salad looks stunning, with its many shades of green, and the chlorophyll-rich matcha green tea powder makes a deliciously healthy addition to the creamy tahini-based dressing.

Prep: 25 mins

180 g (6¼ oz) spinach leaves

3 asparagus spears, shaved into ribbons

75 g (2½ oz) pomegranate arils (see tip, page 40)

150 g (5 oz) shelled fresh peas (or frozen and thawed)

FOR THE CREAMY MATCHA DRESSING

2 tablespoons tahini

1 teaspoon matcha powder

2 tablespoons lemon juice

2 tablespoons water

1 tablespoon liquid aminos

pinch of salt

1 Toss the spinach and asparagus ribbons together in a bowl or on a serving platter. Top with the pomegranate arils and peas.

2 For the matcha dressing, whisk together the ingredients in a small bowl until smooth. If the dressing is too thick, add 1 teaspoon of water at a time until thin enough to drizzle over the top of the salad.

CALORIES (PER SERVING)	109
PROTEIN	6.5 G
TOTAL FAT	4.7 G
SATURATED FAT	0.7 G
CARBOHYDRATES	37.9 G
DIETARY FIBRE	5.9 G
SUGARS	5.4 G
VITAMINS	A, C

WARM SPINACH, QUINOA AND SHIITAKE SALAD

Serves 4
gluten-free

Warm, chewy shiitake mushrooms lend a 'meatiness' to this salad. It can be served as an iron-rich side, thanks to the spinach — or double the quantity of quinoa and serve as two larger portions for a main meal.

Prep: 5 mins | Cook: 25 mins

200 g (7 oz) shiitake mushrooms

1 tablespoon extra-virgin olive oil

2 garlic cloves, minced

2 tablespoons lime juice

2 tablespoons gluten-free hoisin sauce

185 g (6½ oz) cooked quinoa

120 g (4¼ oz) baby spinach

1 tablespoon toasted sesame oil

1 tablespoon gluten-free tamari

See image, opposite, front

1 Clean the mushrooms and trim their ends. In a non-stick frying pan, heat the oil over a medium-high heat, then add the garlic and mushrooms and sauté for 5 to 7 minutes, or until the juices are released.

2 In a small bowl, whisk together the lime juice and hoisin sauce. Add this to the frying pan and stir well, coating the mushrooms and cooking for another minute, though don't cook off the liquid as this will be the dressing.

3 Gently re-heat the quinoa if it's not already warm and toss with the spinach in a salad bowl. Add the sautéed mushrooms, reserving the liquid in the pan.

4 Add the sesame oil and tamari to the juices in the pan and whisk to combine. Drizzle over the salad and serve warm.

CALORIES (PER SERVING)	131
PROTEIN	3.5 G
TOTAL FAT	6.1 G
SATURATED FAT	0.8 G
CARBOHYDRATES	17.7 G
DIETARY FIBRE	2.5 G
SUGARS	3 G
VITAMINS	A, C

CAPRESE-STUFFED GRILLED AVOCADO

Serves 4
gluten-free

Carotenoid-dense avocados and marinated tofu take the place of cheese in this satisfying salad, heightening its anti-inflammatory properties.

Prep: 10 mins (plus 1–8 hrs' marinating) | Cook: 6 mins

60 g (2 oz) Pepita Pesto (page 99)

2 tablespoons extra-virgin olive oil

60 g (2 oz) cubed firm tofu (0.5-cm/¼-inch cubes)

2 avocados

150 g (5 oz) halved cherry tomatoes

pinch of salt

See image, page 52, left

1 In a small bowl, mix the pesto with the olive oil. Pour half of this mixture over the cubed tofu, tossing to coat all the pieces. Cover with cling film and set aside to marinate in the fridge for at least an hour, or ideally overnight. Store the remaining pesto in the fridge for later use.

2 Once the tofu has marinated, slice the avocados in half lengthways and carefully remove the pits. Using a large spoon, gently scoop out each half, being careful to keep it intact.

3 Brush a griddle pan generously with oil and place the avocado halves cut-side down to cook for 5 to 6 minutes, until warmed. Remove (gently as the avocado is tender) and place on serving plates, grilled-side up.

4 Remove the tofu from the fridge and toss with the tomatoes and the remaining pesto sauce. Spoon into the cavity of each avocado, piling it high. Sprinkle with a pinch of salt, and serve.

CALORIES (PER SERVING)	358
PROTEIN	6.2 G
TOTAL FAT	34.2 G
SATURATED FAT	6.6 G
CARBOHYDRATES	11.6 G
DIETARY FIBRE	7.7 G
SUGARS	2.6 G
VITAMINS	B6, C, E

AVOCADO-MASSAGED KALE SALAD

Serves 4
gluten-free

I could eat kale massaged with avocado several times a week, but add a superfood salad topper as a wholesome, crunchy garnish and I'll eat it every day.

Prep: 15 mins | Cook: 10 mins

1 bunch kale (about 10–12 stalks)

1 avocado

1 tablespoon lemon juice, plus extra for drizzling

½ x 350 g (12 oz) package extra-firm tofu (optional)

olive oil

sea salt and freshly ground black pepper, to taste

FOR THE SUPERFOOD TOPPER

2 tablespoons amaranth

40 g (1½ oz) sesame seeds

35 g (1¼ oz) shelled hemp seeds

75 g (2½ oz) pumpkin seeds

1 teaspoon extra-virgin olive oil

¼ teaspoon each of sea salt, pepper, garlic powder, thyme

See image, page 52, rear

CALORIES (PER SERVING)	397
PROTEIN	17.2 G
TOTAL FAT	30.8 G
SATURATED FAT	5.4 G
CARBOHYDRATES	19.3 G
DIETARY FIBRE	7.6 G
SUGARS	1.1 G
VITAMINS	A, C, E

1 Wash and dry the kale leaves. Remove the tough stems (page 17), tear the leaves into bite-sized pieces and place in a large salad bowl. Scoop out the flesh of the avocado and add to the bowl. Using clean hands, massage the avocado into the greens, squeezing, mashing and mixing as you go. This should take about a minute or so. Season lightly with the lemon juice and a little salt.

2 For the superfood topper, heat a small saucepan with a tight-fitting lid over a medium-high heat. To check that it's hot enough, drop in a little water – it should sizzle and evaporate straight away. Add 1 tablespoon of the amaranth seeds to the saucepan, cover immediately and begin shaking the saucepan back and forth quickly to keep the amaranth moving for 15 seconds. Remove from the heat. At least half (hopefully all) of the grains will have popped. Transfer these to a bowl, return the pan to the heat and repeat with the remaining amaranth seeds, then add the other seeds to the bowl.

3 Return the saucepan to a medium heat and add the oil. Add the seeds to the oil and stir to coat using a wooden spoon. Sprinkle in the seasonings and continue to stir over a medium heat for 5 minutes. Remove from the heat to cool fully.

4 If using the tofu, cut it into 0.5-cm (¼-inch) thick pieces. Press the pieces inside a clean tea towel folded over on itself to remove any excess water. Place the tofu in a shallow dish where it can lay flat, drizzle with a little lemon juice and season with salt and pepper. Heat a frying pan over a medium-high heat and add a little olive oil. Heat for 10 seconds, then place the tofu in the frying pan. Sear for 2 minutes, then flip and repeat on the other side until heated through and the tofu has browned lightly.

5 Place the massaged leaves onto serving plates and top with the salad topper and tofu, if using.

VIETNAMESE BRUSSELS SPROUT AND NOODLE SALAD

This fresh and crunchy salad is bound to fill you up and brighten your day, with vitamin C-rich Brussels sprouts and lively flavours from heaps of fresh herbs.

Prep: 15 mins | Cook: 5 mins

180 g (6¼ oz) Brussels sprouts

300 g (10½ oz) bean sprouts

1 large carrot, julienned

25 g (¾ oz) Thai basil

25 g (¾ oz) coriander

10 g (¼ oz) mint

75 g (2½ oz) dry-roasted peanuts, chopped

100 g (3½ oz) rice vermicelli noodles

3 tablespoons lime juice

2 tablespoons gluten-free tamari or light soya sauce

2 teaspoons water

2 teaspoons rice vinegar

1 teaspoon unrefined cane sugar

1 small Thai chilli, minced, or ½ teaspoon dried chilli flakes (optional)

1 Peel away and discard the outer leaves of the Brussels sprouts. Rinse the sprouts well and pat dry. Slice each one in half, then, cut-side down, slice into thin ribbons. Transfer to a bowl and add the bean sprouts and carrot.

2 Roughly chop the fresh herbs and add these to the bowl, along with the peanuts.

3 Prepare the rice noodles according to the packet instructions. If they are very long, cut them in half to make tossing and serving the salad easier. Add to the salad bowl.

4 In a small bowl, whisk the remaining ingredients together, toss through the salad, and serve.

CALORIES (PER SERVING)	178
PROTEIN	8.5 G
TOTAL FAT	6.4 G
SATURATED FAT	0.9 G
CARBOHYDRATES	24 G
DIETARY FIBRE	3.1 G
SUGARS	2.7 G
VITAMINS	A, C

APPLE, BEETROOT, BROCCOLI SLAW

Serves 6
gluten-free

This beautiful salad is full of good-for-you ingredients, including broccoli stalks. One taste of this slaw and you'll never toss those delicious (and nutritious) stalks into the compost again.

Prep: 20 mins

3 yellow beetroot, peeled

1 tart apple (such as Granny Smith), peeled and cored

2 large broccoli stalks, peeled and trimmed (at the base)

160 g (5¼ oz) cooked chickpeas

FOR THE CREAMY TURMERIC DRESSING

2 tablespoons tahini

1 teaspoon turmeric

2 tablespoons lemon juice

2 tablespoons water

1 tablespoon liquid aminos

pinch of salt

1 To shred or julienne the beetroot, apple and broccoli, use a food processor fitted with a grating attachment, a microplane fitted with a julienne blade, or do it by hand with a knife. Place the shredded fruit and veggies into a salad bowl with the chickpeas.

2 For the dressing, whisk together the ingredients in a small bowl until smooth. If the dressing is too thick, add 1 teaspoon of water at a time until thin enough to drizzle over and toss through the salad in the bowl. Serve immediately or refrigerate until ready to eat.

CALORIES (PER SERVING)	119
PROTEIN	4.8 G
TOTAL FAT	3.7 G
SATURATED FAT	0.5 G
CARBOHYDRATES	35.5 G
DIETARY FIBRE	4.7 G
SUGARS	8.8 G
VITAMINS	B6, C

PICNIC SWEET POTATO SALAD

Traditional potato salad gets a superfood injection of sweet potatoes here, adding another layer of flavour as well as loads of vitamin C. Any leftovers are perfect for lunch on-the-go the next day.

Prep: 20 mins | Cook: 20 mins

2 large sweet potatoes
2 medium potatoes
120 g (4¼ oz) diced celery
120 g (4¼ oz) diced onion
5–10 g (⅛–¼ oz) dill, chopped
1 large dill pickle, finely diced
sea salt and freshly ground black pepper, to taste

FOR THE DRESSING

125 ml (4½ fl oz) vegan mayonnaise
1 tablespoon extra-virgin olive oil
1 tablespoon Dijon mustard
½ tablespoon lemon juice
½ tablespoon dill pickle juice

See image, opposite, front

1 Peel all the potatoes and cut into bite-sized pieces. Steam them over a pot of boiling salted water until fork tender, about 15 to 20 minutes. Remove from the heat and leave to cool, then transfer to a salad bowl and chill for 20 minutes.

2 For the dressing, place all the ingredients in a food processor and blend until smooth, scraping down the edges as you go.

3 Add the celery, onions, dill and pickle to the potatoes. Toss the dressing through the salad, season with salt and pepper, and serve. This salad can be made a day ahead and kept in the fridge until ready to serve.

CALORIES (PER SERVING)	228
PROTEIN	3.3 G
TOTAL FAT	7.4 G
SATURATED FAT	0 G
CARBOHYDRATES	38.4 G
DIETARY FIBRE	6.2 G
SUGARS	3 G
VITAMINS	C

SOUTH-WESTERN SALAD

Serves 6
gluten-free

A wonderfully vibrant, colourful salad with a tangy citrus dressing, packed with immune-boosting vitamin C.

Prep: 15 mins | Cook: 10 mins

2 cobs of corn, shucked

1 x 400 g (14 oz) tin black beans, drained and rinsed

1 red pepper, diced

60 g (2 oz) diced red onion

25 g (¾ oz) coriander, chopped

1 romaine heart, chopped

¾ avocado, cubed

FOR THE LIME VINAIGRETTE

3 tablespoons lime juice

3 tablespoons extra-virgin olive oil or flax oil

½ garlic clove, minced

1 teaspoon ground cumin

1 teaspoon sea salt

¼ teaspoon oregano

See image, page 61, rear

1 Cook the corn under a grill at medium heat for 7 to 10 minutes, turning every 2 minutes, until lightly browned. Set aside until cool enough to handle, then remove the kernels from the cobs using a sharp knife. Transfer to a bowl.

2 Add the remaining salad ingredients to the bowl and mix gently to combine.

3 For the vinaigrette, whisk together all the ingredients until combined. Dress the salad just before serving.

VARIATION: The salad also makes a killer burrito filling; try rolling it up in a brown rice or flour tortilla for a midweek meal.

CALORIES (PER SERVING)	187
PROTEIN	6.3 G
TOTAL FAT	6.8 G
SATURATED FAT	1.3 G
CARBOHYDRATES	27.4 G
DIETARY FIBRE	7.2 G
SUGARS	4.4 G
VITAMINS	A, C

GOJI BERRY CONFETTI SALAD

This colourful salad has been showered with superfood sprinkles! Every bite is full of flavour, texture and powerful goji amino acids and vitamins. A good one to make ahead and keep in the fridge for a healthy addition to a lunchbox.

Prep: 15 mins | Cook: 10 mins

170 g (5¾ oz) quinoa
440 ml (15 fl oz) water
1 large carrot, grated
2 celery stalks, diced
1 yellow pepper, seeded and diced
100 g (3½ oz) shelled fresh peas
(or frozen and thawed)
60 g (2 oz) goji berries
5 g (⅛ oz) parsley, finely chopped
juice of 1 lemon
2 tablespoons extra-virgin olive oil
sea salt, to taste

See image, page 135, rear

1 Rinse the quinoa well in a fine mesh sieve. In a small saucepan, bring the quinoa and water to a boil, then reduce the heat to a low simmer, cover, and cook for 15 minutes or until all the liquid has been absorbed. Remove from the heat and leave, covered, for an additional 5 minutes. Fluff with a fork and transfer to a large bowl to cool for 10 minutes.

2 Fold in the carrot, celery, pepper, peas, goji berries and parsley.

3 In a small bowl, whisk together the lemon juice, olive oil and salt. Pour over the quinoa and toss to combine. Store any leftovers in a covered container in the fridge for up to five days.

SUPERFOOD TIP: Goji berries can be fairly dry, much more so than raisins. They will soften up in the salad over the course of a few hours, however they can be given a 10-minute soak in warm water before using, if preferred.

CALORIES (PER SERVING)	207
PROTEIN	5.6 G
TOTAL FAT	7.1 G
SATURATED FAT	1 G
CARBOHYDRATES	30.9 G
DIETARY FIBRE	4.6 G
SUGARS	9.3 G
VITAMINS	A, B6, C

SWEET POTATO, BRUSSELS SPROUT AND BARLEY SOUP

Serves 6
gluten-free

This soup is so full of vegetables, grains and pulses that each bowl is an entire meal in itself. For me, the stars of the soup are the Brussels sprouts, tasting delicious and offering protection from vitamin A deficiency and cardiovascular diseases.

Prep: 10 mins | Cook: 50 mins

2 tablespoons extra-virgin olive oil

60 g (2 oz) diced onion or shallots

1 courgette, sliced into half moons

260 g (9¼ oz) cubed sweet potato

140 g (4¾ oz) halved Brussels sprouts

1 teaspoon dried basil

½ teaspoon dried rosemary

1 x 400 g (14 oz) tin diced tomatoes

320 g (11¼ oz) cooked or tinned chickpeas

1 litre (35 fl oz) vegetable broth

1 litre (35 fl oz) water

220 g (7¾ oz) pot barley

2 tablespoons liquid aminos

sea salt and freshly ground black pepper, to taste

1 In a large pot, heat the olive oil over a medium heat, then sauté the shallots until softened, about 3 to 4 minutes. Add all the vegetables and herbs and stir to coat in the oil. Add the tomatoes and chickpeas and stir to combine.

2 Add the broth, water, barley and liquid aminos and bring to a boil. Reduce the heat and simmer, covered, for 35 to 40 minutes, or until the barley is tender. Be sure to give the soup a good stir every 10 minutes or so, and add more liquid if necessary to achieve your preferred consistency. Season to taste, and serve with warm, crusty bread.

CALORIES (PER SERVING)	365
PROTEIN	14.7 G
TOTAL FAT	7.8 G
SATURATED FAT	1.2 G
CARBOHYDRATES	95.6 G
DIETARY FIBRE	13.9 G
SUGARS	11 G
VITAMINS	B6, C

COCONUT KALE SOUP WITH CASHEW 'CRÈME FRAÎCHE'

Serves 4–6
gluten-free

A bright-green soup full of kale, to pump you up with plenty of fibre, protein and bone-strengthening calcium. Rich, comforting and creamy.

Prep: 10 mins | Cook: 30 mins

1 tablespoon coconut oil
120 g (4¼ oz) chopped onion
425 g (15 oz) chopped kale
1 litre (35 fl oz) vegetable broth
290 g (10¼ oz) shelled peas
1 small potato, peeled and cubed
1 x 400 g (14 oz) tin light coconut milk
sea salt and freshly ground black pepper, to taste
extra-virgin olive oil or hemp oil, to serve

FOR THE CASHEW 'CRÈME FRAÎCHE'
85 g (3 oz) raw cashews, soaked for 4 to 6 hours
1 teaspoon lemon juice
1 teaspoon maple syrup
2–3 tablespoons water

See image, opposite, front

1 Heat the coconut oil in a medium saucepan over a medium-high heat, then add the onions and sauté for 4 to 5 minutes, or until they're soft and just beginning to lightly brown.

2 Add the kale and 250 ml (9 fl oz) of broth and cook for 2 minutes, stirring constantly. Add the peas, potato and the remaining broth and increase the heat, bringing the soup to a boil. Reduce the heat to medium and cook, uncovered, for 12 to 15 minutes.

3 Using an immersion blender, or a regular blender (in batches), purée the soup until smooth; a high-powered blender is best for getting it silky-smooth. Return to the saucepan, stir in the coconut milk and season to taste. Keep warm on the hob until ready to serve.

4 For the cashew 'crème fraîche', place all the ingredients in a food processor and blend until creamy and pourable. Serve the soup in bowls with a drizzle of cashew crème fraîche and a few drops of high-quality olive or hemp oil.

CALORIES (PER SERVING)	306
PROTEIN	13.7 G
TOTAL FAT	15.9 G
SATURATED FAT	6.9 G
CARBOHYDRATES	27 G
DIETARY FIBRE	5.2 G
SUGARS	7.8 G
VITAMINS	A, C

BEETROOT AND ACAI BORSCHT

Serves 6
gluten-free

Borscht is a vibrant, healthy option full of beetroot, carrots and potassium-rich cabbage, but an added hint of acai gives it those extra antioxidant superpowers.

Prep: 20 mins | Cook: 35 mins

2 carrots
4 beetroot
½ head green cabbage
2 tablespoons coconut oil
1 small onion, diced
2 garlic cloves, pressed
750 ml (26½ fl oz) vegetable broth
500 ml (18 fl oz) water
juice of 1 lemon
3 tablespoons liquid aminos
1 x 100 g (3½ oz) packet acai purée
sea salt and freshly ground black pepper, to taste
vegan sour cream or Cashew 'Crème Fraîche' (page 66), to serve

See image, page 67, rear

1 To shred or grate the carrots, beetroot and cabbage, use a food processor fitted with a grating attachment, a box grater, or do it by hand with a knife.

2 In a large pot, heat the oil over a medium heat, then add the onion and garlic and sauté for 2 minutes, until softened. Add the grated vegetables, increase the heat to medium-high and cook for 5 minutes, stirring often, until they have softened and begun to cook down.

3 Add the broth, water, lemon juice and liquid aminos to the pot and bring to a simmer. Reduce the heat to low, stir well, then cover and leave to simmer for 25 minutes.

4 Remove half of the soup to a bowl and set aside to cool. Add the acai purée to the cooled soup in the bowl, then carefully blend this half of the soup in a blender (in batches), or using an immersion blender, returning it to the pot once smooth.

5 Season to taste and serve with a dollop of vegan sour cream or cashew 'crème fraîche'.

CALORIES (PER SERVING)	132
PROTEIN	5.1 G
TOTAL FAT	6.8 G
SATURATED FAT	5.1 G
CARBOHYDRATES	64.5 G
DIETARY FIBRE	4.1 G
SUGARS	9.6 G
VITAMINS	A, C

CARROT, APPLE AND GINGER SOUP

Serves 4
gluten-free

Subtly sweet from the vitamin-rich apple, with a spicy, antibacterial ginger kick.

Prep: 15 mins | Cook: 40 mins

1 tablespoon extra-virgin olive oil

2 shallots, diced

2 tablespoons minced fresh ginger

520 g (18¼ oz) chopped carrots

1 apple, peeled, cored, chopped

750 ml (26½ fl oz) vegetable broth

sea salt and freshly ground black pepper, to taste

chives, to serve

25 g (¾ oz) chopped walnuts, toasted, to serve (optional)

See image, page 67, left

1 In a large pot, heat the oil over a medium heat, then add the shallots and sauté for 5 minutes, until soft. Add the ginger, carrots and apple and continue to sauté for another 5 minutes. Add the broth to the pot, bring to a boil, then reduce the heat and simmer for 25 to 30 minutes, until the carrots are soft.

2 Using a blender, purée the soup until smooth. Season to taste, ladle into bowls, and top with the chives and walnuts.

CALORIES (PER SERVING)	175
PROTEIN	6.5 G
TOTAL FAT	8.5 G
SATURATED FAT	1.1 G
CARBOHYDRATES	20 G
DIETARY FIBRE	4.4 G
SUGARS	10 G
VITAMINS	A, B6

GARLIC AND GINGER LENTIL SOUP

Serves 6
gluten-free

A cosy soup inspired by my grandmother Doris's family-favourite recipe.

Prep: 15 mins | Cook: 1 hr 15 mins

60 ml (2 fl oz) extra-virgin olive oil

1 small onion, chopped

2 garlic cloves, minced

2 tablespoons minced fresh ginger

1 teaspoon turmeric

1 teaspoon ground cumin

200 g (7 oz) red lentils, rinsed

100 g (3½ oz) chopped carrots

1 x 400 g (14 oz) tin salt-free diced tomatoes

sea salt and freshly ground black pepper, to taste

See image, page 71, rear

1 Heat the oil in a medium saucepan over a medium heat, then add the onion, garlic and ginger and sauté for 5 minutes, stirring, until the onions have softened. Add the spices, lentils, carrots and tomatoes, stirring well. Slowly pour in 750 ml (26½ fl oz) of water and stir again.

2 Bring to a boil, then cover and reduce the heat to low. Simmer for 1 hour, stirring occasionally, then season to taste and serve.

CALORIES (PER SERVING)	235
PROTEIN	9.2 G
TOTAL FAT	10 G
SATURATED FAT	1.4 G
CARBOHYDRATES	25.1 G
DIETARY FIBRE	11.3 G
SUGARS	2.3 G
VITAMINS	A

ADZUKI BEAN AND PUMPKIN CHILLI

Serves 6
gluten-free

This is the kind of chilli to stick to your ribs on a cold winter's day. It's smoky, satisfying and thick, thanks to the creamy pumpkin purée. Make a double batch and fill your freezer with single portions for quick, no-fuss meals.

Prep: 10 mins | Cook: 1 hr

1 tablespoon coconut oil

1 onion, diced

3 celery stalks, diced

2 carrots, diced

2 teaspoons sea salt

2 teaspoons chilli powder

1 teaspoon ground cumin

½ teaspoon garlic powder

½ teaspoon smoked paprika

¼ teaspoon cinnamon

1 x 400 g (14 oz) tin adzuki beans, drained and rinsed

330 g (11½ oz) pumpkin purée (page 17), or tinned pumpkin

1 x 800 g (28 oz) tin diced tomatoes

See image, opposite, front

1 In a large pot or Dutch oven, heat the coconut oil over a medium heat, then add the onion, celery and carrots and sauté until fragrant and beginning to soften, about 5 to 7 minutes.

2 Add the salt and spices to the pot, along with the beans, pumpkin purée and diced tomatoes, and stir well. Increase the heat to high and bring to a boil, then reduce the heat to medium-low and cook, covered, for 35 to 40 minutes, stirring occasionally, until the carrots are tender. Serve with brown rice, quinoa or tortilla chips.

CALORIES (PER SERVING)	255
PROTEIN	5.3 G
TOTAL FAT	2.6 G
SATURATED FAT	2 G
CARBOHYDRATES	53.1 G
DIETARY FIBRE	4.3 G
SUGARS	7.4 G
VITAMINS	A

HERBALICIOUS HEMP GAZPACHO

Serve this raw, chilled soup in the summer and let garlic's potent selenium content and hemp's omega-rich, heart-healthy benefits cool you down.

**Prep: 20 mins
(plus 2–3 hrs' chilling)**

1 English cucumber, peeled and diced

2 vine-ripened tomatoes, diced

1 yellow pepper, seeded and diced

3 garlic cloves, minced

2 tablespoons chopped chives, plus 1 teaspoon to serve

5 g (⅛ oz) basil, chopped

5 g (⅛ oz) parsley, chopped

½ small red onion, chopped

750 ml (26½ fl oz) low-sodium tomato juice

50 g (1¾ oz) shelled hemp seeds, plus 1 tablespoon to serve

sea salt and freshly ground black pepper, to taste

1 In a large bowl, combine the cucumber, tomatoes and pepper.

2 Remove 350 g (12¼ oz) of the vegetable mixture from the bowl and place in a blender along with the garlic, herbs, onion, 250 ml (9 fl oz) of tomato juice and hemp seeds. Blend until smooth. Return this purée to the bowl, along with the remaining tomato juice, stir well, and season to taste.

3 Chill for 2 to 3 hours in the fridge before serving. Top with a sprinkling of hemp seeds and chives.

CALORIES (PER SERVING)	126
PROTEIN	7.2 G
TOTAL FAT	7.2 G
SATURATED FAT	0.7 G
CARBOHYDRATES	10.4 G
DIETARY FIBRE	1.9 G
SUGARS	5.9 G
VITAMINS	A, C

UDON SOUP WITH BROCCOLI, KALE AND SWEET POTATO

Serves 4
gluten-free
option

An Asian-inspired noodle broth boasting loads of calcium and chlorophyll, and the addition of magnesium-rich, relaxation-inducing sweet potato. If you love greens as much as I do, you can also up the quantity of kale! For a gluten-free option, use gluten-free udon noodles.

Prep: 15 mins | Cook: 20 mins

½ tablespoon coconut oil

1 garlic clove, minced

125 g (4½ oz) cubed sweet potato
(2.5-cm/½-inch cubes)

1 litre (35 fl oz) water

1 litre (35 fl oz) vegetable broth

3 tablespoons gluten-free tamari

1 tablespoon sesame oil

1 teaspoon Sriracha or garlic chilli
sauce

400 g (14 oz) udon noodles

180 g (6¼ oz) mini chopped
broccoli florets

75 g (2½ oz) kale

sesame seeds, to serve

10 g (¼ oz) coriander, chopped,
to serve

1 In a medium saucepan, heat the oil over a medium heat, then add the garlic and sweet potato and sauté until the garlic is fragrant and cooked, but not yet browned. Stir well to coat the sweet potato in the oil.

2 Slowly add the water and broth to the saucepan, and bring to a simmer. Reduce the heat to low and continue to simmer, covered, for 10 to 15 minutes. Check that the sweet potato is cooked through (it should be very soft), then add all the remaining ingredients, except for the kale, and increase the heat to medium. Cook for a final 3 minutes, until the noodles are tender and the broccoli is bright green with a slight crunch.

3 Wash and dry the kale leaves. Remove the tough stems (page 17) and finely slice the leaves. Stir into the saucepan, and let it wilt for 1 minute. Ladle the soup into bowls, top with a sprinkling of sesame seeds and coriander, and serve.

CALORIES (PER SERVING)	320
PROTEIN	14.7 G
TOTAL FAT	5.7 G
SATURATED FAT	1.4 G
CARBOHYDRATES	53.7 G
DIETARY FIBRE	5.4 G
SUGARS	8 G
VITAMINS	A, C

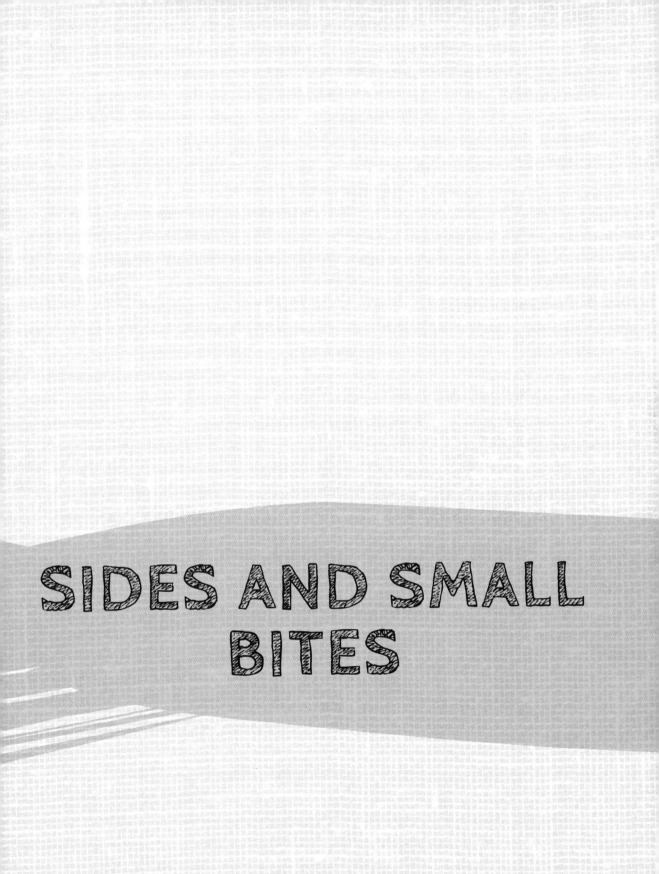

SIDES AND SMALL BITES

TURMERIC-ROASTED CAULIFLOWER STEAKS

Serves 3–4
gluten-free

Cauliflower can masquerade as many things — in this case it's cut into thick steaks, a beautiful accompaniment to any meal. Superfood duo turmeric and ginger work their anti-inflammatory magic here, too.

Prep: 15 mins | Cook: 35 mins

1 large head cauliflower
1 tablespoon coconut oil
1 tablespoon turmeric
1 tablespoon minced fresh ginger
½ tablespoon lemon juice
sea salt and freshly ground black pepper, to taste
chopped coriander or parsley, to serve

1 Preheat the oven to 220°C (425°F). Line a baking sheet with baking paper.

2 Trim the greens from the cauliflower head. Soak the head in warm water for 10 minutes, then turn it upside down in a sieve to drip dry. Remove from the sieve, stand it upright on its stem, and slice into 2–2.5-cm (¾–1-inch) slices. The outer slices will crumble (save these florets for another use), but ideally you will be left with four 'steaks'. Remove any remaining leaves and trim the stem end of the cauliflower, leaving the core intact.

3 In a shallow dish, combine the oil, turmeric, ginger, lemon juice and a little seasoning. Dip the cauliflower steaks in the sauce, flipping over to cover both sides; you may want to wear gloves or your hands will be yellow for a few days!

4 Place the slices of cauliflower on the lined baking sheet and roast for 25 to 35 minutes, gently turning after 20 minutes, until the stems are fork tender and golden brown. Sprinkle with coriander or parsley and serve with a grain and salad for a complete meal.

CALORIES (PER SERVING)	76
PROTEIN	3.1 G
TOTAL FAT	3.8 G
SATURATED FAT	3.1 G
CARBOHYDRATES	9.7 G
DIETARY FIBRE	4.1 G
SUGARS	3.6 G
VITAMINS	B6, C

SUPER SEEDY QUINOA FLATBREADS

Serves 6–8
gluten-free

These cracker-like flatbreads are a one-bowl breeze to make, and the result is wholesome, crunchy and perfect for dipping in hummus or chilli, or for spreading with seed or nut butters.

Prep: 10 mins | Cook: 55 mins

170 g (5¾ oz) quinoa flakes
25 g (¾ oz) ground flax meal
40 g (1½ oz) chia seeds
2 tablespoons amaranth
2 tablespoons sesame seeds
¼ teaspoon dried basil
¼ teaspoon oregano
¼ teaspoon onion powder
¼ teaspoon garlic powder
½ teaspoon sea salt
335 ml (11¼ fl oz) water

See image, page 76, rear

1 Preheat the oven to 160°C (325°F). Line a baking sheet with baking paper.

2 In a large bowl, mix all the ingredients together and set aside. After 10 minutes, stir again; the mixture will be thick but spreadable.

3 Spread the mixture over the baking sheet, using a silicone spatula to get it thin and even all the way to the edges. If it's not rolled thin enough, the flatbreads won't crisp up and will be more like bread or a wrap (though equally delicious!). If desired, sprinkle over an additional few pinches of sea salt. Bake for 30 to 40 minutes, until it's hard enough that you can peel it off and it will stay together.

4 Remove from the oven, cool for a few minutes, and roughly slice or break into pieces. Flip the pieces over on the sheet and bake for another 10 to 15 minutes, until perfectly crisp. Leave to cool fully, then store in an airtight container for up to four days.

CALORIES (PER SERVING)	140
PROTEIN	5.1
TOTAL FAT	4.5
SATURATED FAT	0.6
CARBOHYDRATES	21
DIETARY FIBRE	4.8
SUGARS	0
VITAMINS	B6

LENTIL HUMMUS

Serves 6–8
gluten-free

One can never have too many hummus recipes in their arsenal. The lentils make this cumin-scented version rich in iron, protein and dietary fibre.

Prep: 5 mins | Cook: 40 mins

200 g (7 oz) dried brown or green lentils, rinsed
750 ml (26½ fl oz) water
2 tablespoons extra-virgin olive oil
2 tablespoons apple cider vinegar
1 tablespoon tahini
1 small shallot, minced
½ teaspoon ground cumin
sea salt and freshly ground black pepper, to taste

See image, page 76, left

1 Bring the lentils and water to a boil in a large pot over a medium heat. Reduce heat to low and cook for 30 to 35 minutes, or until the lentils are tender. Drain and leave to cool.

2 Combine the lentils with the remaining ingredients in a food processor and process until smooth. A little water can be added to thin the hummus, if required. Season to taste.

CALORIES (PER SERVING)	120
PROTEIN	5.9
TOTAL FAT	4.8
SATURATED FAT	0.6
CARBOHYDRATES	13.4
DIETARY FIBRE	2.4
SUGARS	0
VITAMINS	B1, B6, E

SUNFLOWER SEED PÂTÉ

Serves 6
gluten-free

Rich and savoury, this tangy, protein-packed pâté is perfect for spreading on crackers or Super Seedy Quinoa Flatbreads (opposite), or as a dip for veggies.

Prep: 40 mins

140 g (4¾ oz) raw sunflower seeds
2 tablespoons chopped sundried tomatoes (dry-packed, not in oil)
60 ml (2 fl oz) water (just boiled)
30 g (1 oz) grated carrot
1 small garlic clove
2 teaspoons apple cider vinegar
¼ teaspoon turmeric
¼ teaspoon ground cumin
sea salt and freshly ground black pepper, to taste
See image, page 76, front

1 Soak the sunflower seeds in water for 30 minutes. Drain and discard the soaking water. Meanwhile, rehydrate the sundried tomatoes in the hot water for 15 minutes. Drain and reserve the soaking water.

2 Place all the ingredients in a food processor with ½ teaspoon of sea salt, and process, adding the soaking water from the tomatoes as needed to achieve a spreadable pâté. Season to taste.

CALORIES (PER SERVING)	143
PROTEIN	5.1
TOTAL FAT	12.1
SATURATED FAT	1.0
CARBOHYDRATES	6.1
DIETARY FIBRE	2.3
SUGARS	1.3
VITAMINS	A, B6

CURRIED LENTIL-WALNUT SLIDERS

Serves 8
gluten-free
option

When mixed together, ground lentils and walnuts have a 'meaty' texture, with all the protein and fibre your body needs. These mini sliders are spicy, sweet and tangy and topped with a fresh, crunchy salsa. For a gluten-free option, use gluten-free buns.

Prep: 10 mins | Cook: 20 mins

75 g (2½ oz) cooked lentils (brown, French or puy)

100 g (3½ oz) walnuts

1 teaspoon curry powder

½ tablespoon liquid aminos

2 tablespoons mango chutney, plus extra to serve (optional)

8 mini slider buns

FOR THE SALSA

1 mango, peeled and diced

75 g (2½ oz) edamame beans

50 g (1¾ oz) diced, seeded cucumber

squeeze of lime juice

pinch of chilli flakes

1 Preheat the oven to 200°C (400°F). Line a baking sheet with baking paper.

2 Place the lentils and walnuts in a food processor and process to a chunky mixture. Remove to a bowl and mix in the curry powder, liquid aminos and mango chutney by hand.

3 Form the mixture into eight equal patties and place on the baking sheet. Bake for 20 minutes, flipping the patties after about 12 minutes, until they are lightly browned on both sides.

4 For the salsa, combine all the ingredients in a food processor and pulse just a few times to chop finely.

5 Serve the sliders on buns with salsa and any other toppings you desire. Another smear of tangy mango chutney is perfect.

CALORIES (PER SERVING)	200
PROTEIN	5.6 G
TOTAL FAT	9.7 G
SATURATED FAT	0.9 G
CARBOHYDRATES	29.3 G
DIETARY FIBRE	3.8 G
SUGARS	7.7 G
VITAMINS	C

QUINOA SUSHI HAND ROLLS

Serves 2–4
gluten-free

These hand rolls make for a great snack or light meal. Full of avocado, quinoa, hemp seeds and raw vegetables, they're surprisingly filling, too. The nori sheets become soggy as they sit, so the rolls are best enjoyed as soon as they're made.

Prep: 15 mins | Cook: 20 mins (or see tip)

1 avocado

2 teaspoons lemon juice

2 teaspoons seasoned rice vinegar

280 g (10 oz) cooked quinoa

2 nori sheets, cut in half

¼ English cucumber, julienned

25 g (¾ oz) shredded Brussels sprouts

½ pepper (red, orange or yellow), thinly sliced

35 g (1¼ oz) shelled hemp seeds

See image, opposite, left

1 In a bowl, mash the avocado with the lemon juice and rice vinegar until smooth. Fold in the cooked quinoa and set aside.

2 To assemble, lay the nori sheets on a cutting board or clean surface. Spread the avocado quinoa mixture over the four sheets, on the left-hand third of the sheet only. Place a little cucumber, Brussels sprouts, peppers and hemp seeds over the top of each and roll up into conical hand rolls. Serve immediately.

SUPERFOOD TIP: Cook quinoa in bulk at the beginning of the week and you will have plenty on hand in the days that follow to make meal preparation that much quicker. I generally follow a 1:2 ratio of quinoa to water.

CALORIES (PER SERVING)	228
PROTEIN	6.9 G
TOTAL FAT	15.1 G
SATURATED FAT	2.3 G
CARBOHYDRATES	18.2 G
DIETARY FIBRE	5.5 G
SUGARS	1.4 G
VITAMINS	C

CRISPY AMARANTH-COATED EDAMAME

Serves 4–6
gluten-free
option

Crispy, crunchy, real-food goodness. Popped amaranth is the cutest thing, and still full of its complete protein glory. For a gluten-free option, use polenta or gluten-free panko breadcrumbs in place of the breadcrumbs.

Prep: 10 mins | Cook: 10 mins

50 g (1¾ oz) amaranth
15 g (½ oz) panko breadcrumbs
½ tablespoon kelp granules
2 tablespoons nutritional yeast
zest of 1 lemon
2 flax eggs (page 17)
300 g (10½ oz) frozen, shelled edamame beans, thawed
sea salt and freshly ground black pepper, to taste

See image, page 84, right

1 Preheat the oven to 200°C (400°F). Line a baking sheet with baking paper.

2 Heat a small saucepan with a tight-fitting lid over a medium-high heat. To check that it's hot enough, drop a little water in – it should sizzle and evaporate straight away. Add 1 tablespoon of the amaranth seeds to the saucepan, cover immediately and begin shaking the saucepan back and forth quickly over the burner to keep the amaranth moving (to prevent burning) for 15 seconds. Remove from the heat. At least half (hopefully all) of the grains will have popped. Transfer these to a bowl, return the pan to the heat, and repeat with each remaining tablespoon of amaranth seeds.

3 To the bowl, add the panko breadcrumbs, kelp granules, nutritional yeast, lemon zest, a little sea salt and ground pepper, and stir to combine.

4 Place 150 g (5 oz) of edamame into the flax eggs to coat them, then lift the beans out using a slotted spoon and toss in the amaranth mixture. Using another slotted spoon (or two forks), lift them on to the baking sheet. Repeat with the second cup of edamame. Spread them out in a single layer, with as few touching as possible.

5 Bake for 8 to 10 minutes, until lightly browned, watching closely after 8 minutes to prevent burning. Remove from the oven and leave to cool to room temperature before serving.

CALORIES (PER SERVING)	96
PROTEIN	6.4 G
TOTAL FAT	2.3 G
SATURATED FAT	0 G
CARBOHYDRATES	12.9 G
DIETARY FIBRE	3.7 G
SUGARS	0.6 G
VITAMINS	B6, B12

BAKED AMARANTH FALAFEL BITES

Standard falafel can be fortified with even more calcium, protein and fibre with the addition of amaranth, 'the little seed that could'. For a gluten-free option, use gluten-free panko breadcrumbs.

Prep: 30 mins | Cook: 25 mins

50 g (1¾ oz) amaranth

125 ml (4½ fl oz) vegetable broth

1 x 425 g (15 oz) tin chickpeas, drained and rinsed, or 240 g (8½ oz) cooked chickpeas

1 garlic clove, minced

3 tablespoons panko breadcrumbs

2 tablespoons chopped parsley

2 tablespoons chopped coriander

1 teaspoon lemon zest

sea salt and freshly ground black pepper, to taste

extra-virgin olive oil

pickled turnip (optional)

FOR THE HUMMUS TAHINI SAUCE

125 ml (4½ fl oz) Lentil Hummus (page 81)

1 tablespoon tahini

3 tablespoons water

1 tablespoon lemon juice

See image, page 76, rear

1 Preheat the oven to 190°C (375°F). Line a baking sheet with baking paper.

2 Place the amaranth and broth in a small pot and bring to a boil over a high heat. Reduce heat to low, cover, and cook for 15 to 20 minutes, stirring occasionally, until the broth has been absorbed. Remove from the heat and set aside.

3 Meanwhile, mash the chickpeas roughly with a potato masher or in a food processor. Transfer the chickpeas to a large bowl and mix in the garlic, panko breadcrumbs, parsley, coriander, zest and cooked amaranth. Season to taste, and refrigerate the mixture for 15 to 20 minutes as it will be quite wet.

4 Scoop out 1 tablespoon of the mixture at a time and roll into bite-sized balls, placing them on the lined baking sheet. Brush or spritz with a little oil. Cook for 15 to 20 minutes, or until the falafels are golden brown and crispy.

5 For the hummus tahini sauce, while the falafels are cooking, combine the lentil hummus with the tahini and water in a bowl. Remove the falafels from the oven and serve with the sauce and pickled turnip, if desired.

CALORIES (PER SERVING)	199
PROTEIN	9.1 G
TOTAL FAT	7.7 G
SATURATED FAT	1.1 G
CARBOHYDRATES	23.8 G
DIETARY FIBRE	7.6 G
SUGARS	0.9 G
VITAMINS	B6

GRILLED RADICCHIO WITH ORANGE

Serves 4
gluten-free

Sweet, juicy, immune-boosting oranges sweeten this grilled radicchio dish.

Prep: 15 mins | Cook: 15 mins

2 heads radicchio, quartered

2 tablespoons extra-virgin olive oil

1 orange, peel and pith removed, sliced into 0.5-cm (¼-inch) thick disks

60 ml (2 fl oz) Hemp Dressing (page 49)

35 g (1¼ oz) roasted sunflower seeds

sea salt and freshly ground black pepper, to taste

See image, opposite, front

1 Brush the radicchio quarters with oil and sprinkle with salt and pepper. Place on a heated griddle pan for 3 minutes on each of the three sides, until lightly charred and tender.

2 Arrange the orange and radicchio on a plate, drizzle with the dressing, top with the pumpkin seeds, and serve.

CALORIES (PER SERVING)	219
PROTEIN	7.3 G
TOTAL FAT	17.1 G
SATURATED FAT	2.3 G
CARBOHYDRATES	11.5 G
DIETARY FIBRE	2.6 G
SUGARS	5.1 G
VITAMINS	C

COCONUT CREAMED KALE

Serves 6
gluten-free

These creamy, Southern-style greens are about as rich in vitamins as kale can get.

Prep: 5 mins | Cook: 25 mins

1 tablespoon extra-virgin olive or coconut oil

2 shallots, thinly sliced

2 garlic cloves, minced

2 bunches kale, woody stems removed (see page 17), leaves finely sliced

1 x 400 ml (14 fl oz) tin light coconut milk

¼ teaspoon red pepper flakes

¼ teaspoon nutmeg

sea salt and freshly ground black pepper, to taste

See image, opposite, rear

1 Heat the oil in a frying pan over a medium-high heat. Add the shallots and sauté for 4 to 5 minutes, then add the garlic and sauté for 2 minutes.

2 Add half the kale and stir until wilted, then add the remaining kale, coconut milk, red pepper flakes and nutmeg. Stir well, reduce heat to medium and simmer for 15 minutes, stirring occasionally until the coconut milk has thickened and reduced. Season to taste and serve.

CALORIES (PER SERVING)	168
PROTEIN	2.5 G
TOTAL FAT	15.0 G
SATURATED FAT	10.5 G
CARBOHYDRATES	8.1 G
DIETARY FIBRE	0.8 G
SUGARS	1.7 G
VITAMINS	A, C, K

AMARANTH WITH TURMERIC, CRANBERRY AND ALMONDS

Serves 4
gluten-free

This savoury, polenta-like porridge is a big warm hug in a bowl. The wonderful texture of amaranth, along with its amazing nutritional profile — packed with iron and protein — makes it well worthy of a place at the table.

Prep: 10 mins | Cook: 30 mins

190 g (6¾ oz) amaranth
625 ml (21 fl oz) vegetable broth
1 teaspoon turmeric
15 g (½ oz) nutritional yeast (optional)
40 g (1½ oz) unsweetened dried cranberries
85 g (3 oz) almonds, chopped

1 Place the amaranth and broth in a small pot and bring to a boil over a medium heat. Cover, reduce heat to low and simmer for 20 minutes, stirring occasionally, until the broth has been absorbed. If after 20 minutes it hasn't been absorbed, remove the lid and cook for another 10 minutes, uncovered, stirring often.

2 Whisk in the turmeric and nutritional yeast, if using, for the last 5 minutes' cooking time. Stir in the cranberries and all but 1 tablespoon of almonds while warm. Top with the remaining almonds and serve.

VARIATION: Omit the turmeric and cranberries and try ½ teaspoon of chopped thyme and a small handful of reconstituted dried porcini mushrooms.

CALORIES (PER SERVING)	358
PROTEIN	14.2 G
TOTAL FAT	14.4 G
SATURATED FAT	2.0 G
CARBOHYDRATES	46.1 G
DIETARY FIBRE	12.7 G
SUGARS	3.8 G
VITAMINS	B6

SWEET POTATO AND COCONUT FRIES

Serves 4
gluten-free

Sweet potato and coconut join forces here for an extra-crunchy baked treat that would make any burger complete. Try them paired with the Black Bean Hemp Patties (page 109) for a crowd-pleasing meal.

Prep: 15 mins | Cook: 30 mins

50 g (1¾ oz) unsweetened desiccated coconut
40 g (1½ oz) polenta
1 teaspoon garlic powder
½ teaspoon cinnamon
½ teaspoon paprika
125 ml (4½ fl oz) non-dairy milk (of choice)
2 large sweet potatoes, peeled and cut into French-fry-style lengths
cooking oil spray
sea salt, for sprinkling
See image, page 111

1 Preheat the oven to 190°C (375°F). Line two baking sheets with baking paper.

2 Mix the coconut, polenta and spices in a large ziplock bag. Pour the milk into a shallow bowl.

3 Working with a handful at a time, dip the sweet potatoes into the milk, then let the excess milk drip off and place them in the bag. Shake the bag to coat the fries. Place the coated sweet potato fries on the baking sheet and repeat with the remaining fries. Spritz with cooking oil spray.

4 Place the baking sheets in the oven and bake for 25 to 30 minutes, removing halfway to flip them over. Watch them closely towards the end of cooking to ensure they don't burn. Remove from the oven and, while still hot, sprinkle with salt.

CALORIES (PER SERVING)	187
PROTEIN	2.9 G
TOTAL FAT	9.0 G
SATURATED FAT	7.2 G
CARBOHYDRATES	25.3 G
DIETARY FIBRE	4.9 G
SUGARS	4.8 G
VITAMINS	A

PISTACHIO AND BROCCOLI PILAF

Serves 4
gluten-free
option

Get your calcium and folate fix with this simple side dish of vibrant green broccoli, chewy toasted orzo and crunchy pistachios. For a gluten-free option, use a gluten-free orzo or substitute with long-grain rice.

Prep: 10 mins | Cook: 25 mins

1 tablespoon extra-virgin olive oil
½ small red onion, finely chopped
150 g (5 oz) orzo
500 ml (18 fl oz) vegetable broth
juice and zest of 1 lemon
180 g (6¼ oz) broccoli florets
65 g (2¼ oz) roaasted pistachios

See image, page 94, right

1 Heat the oil in a medium pan over a medium-high heat, add the onion and sauté for 4 to 5 minutes, until softened. Add the orzo for another 2 minutes, stirring well to brown the pasta.

2 Slowly stir in the broth, lemon juice and zest, bring to a boil, cover, reduce the heat and simmer for 15 minutes, until the liquid has been mostly absorbed.

3 Add the broccoli, stir, cover, and cook for another 2 minutes, until the broccoli is lightly steamed but still holds its crunch. Transfer to a serving dish and stir in the pistachios.

VARIATION: Turn this side dish into a glorious salad by tossing it with rocket and baby lettuce greens with an added squeeze of fresh lemon and some extra-virgin olive oil.

CALORIES (PER SERVING)	133
PROTEIN	2.2 G
TOTAL FAT	6.1 G
SATURATED FAT	2.3 G
CARBOHYDRATES	18.6 G
DIETARY FIBRE	2.6 G
SUGARS	6.4 G
VITAMINS	A, B6, C

SWEET POTATOES WITH WALNUTS AND POMEGRANATE

Serves 4–6
gluten-free

These sweet potatoes are not quite candied, but still amazingly sweet thanks to the natural sugars in the orange juice. They are a beautiful, nutritious and yummy addition to any festive table.

Prep: 15 mins | Cook: 35 mins

1 tablespoon melted coconut oil

125 ml (4½ fl oz) freshly squeezed orange juice

½ teaspoon cinnamon

3 medium sweet potatoes, scrubbed and sliced into circles 1.25-cm (½-inch) thick

2 teaspoons orange zest

75 g (2½ oz) pomegranate arils (see tip, page 40)

35 g (1¼ oz) toasted walnuts

sea salt, to taste

See image, opposite, left

1 Preheat the oven to 200°C (400°F). Line two baking sheets with baking paper.

2 In a large bowl, whisk together the oil, juice and cinnamon, then add the sweet potatoes and toss everything together.

3 Spread the potatoes out on the baking sheets, reserving the orange juice mixture. Sprinkle the potatoes with orange zest and a few pinches of sea salt, and bake for 35 minutes, turning once, until golden and cooked through.

4 Remove from the oven, spoon onto a large serving platter, and top with the reserved orange juice mixture, pomegranate arils and walnuts.

CALORIES (PER SERVING)	291
PROTEIN	9.5 G
TOTAL FAT	11.8 G
SATURATED FAT	1.4 G
CARBOHYDRATES	38.1 G
DIETARY FIBRE	5.0 G
SUGARS	5.7 G
VITAMINS	C

GREEN BEANS WITH HEMP AND ALMOND BREADCRUMBS

Serves 6–8
gluten-free

These beans are an homage to my late Grandfather Chaim, who often made green beans with 'breadcrumbs' for Sunday brunch. Here, traditional breadcrumbs are replaced with ground almonds and shelled hemp seeds, providing a gluten-free, protein-rich coating.

Prep: 10 mins | Cook: 15 mins

450 g (1 lb) green beans, trimmed

85 g (3 oz) almonds

3 tablespoons coconut oil or extra-virgin olive oil

3 garlic cloves, minced

75 g (2½ oz) shelled hemp seeds

salt and freshly ground black pepper, to taste

See image, opposite, front right

1 Bring a large pot of salted water to a boil and add the beans. Cook for 3 to 4 minutes, until tender but still a bit crunchy, then drain and run under cold water. Leave to drain in a colander.

2 Grind the almonds in a food processor until they resemble fine breadcrumbs.

3 Heat the oil in a large frying pan over a medium heat and add the garlic, followed by the almond meal and hemp seeds, toasting for 2 to 3 minutes until they begin to brown ever so slightly. Then toss in the beans and cook for another minute. Season to taste and serve. If making in advance, turn off the heat on the breadcrumbs before adding the beans, then simply reheat and add the beans before serving.

SUPERFOOD TIP: If you don't have a food processor, you can use a spice mill for grinding, or use a scant 50 g (1¾ oz) of shop-bought almond meal instead.

CALORIES (PER SERVING)	177
PROTEIN	6.3 G
TOTAL FAT	14.6 G
SATURATED FAT	5.3 G
CARBOHYDRATES	7.2 G
DIETARY FIBRE	3.8 G
SUGARS	1.2 G
VITAMINS	C

COLOURFUL ROASTED POTATOES AND APPLE

A colourful, slightly sweet dish that would be perfect with any autumn meal. It's a nice change from the usual potato side, especially with the addition of roasted apple.

Prep: 15 mins | Cook: 45 mins

2 medium sweet potatoes

2 firm apples (like Fuji)

300 g (10½ oz) mini potatoes (purple or coloured if available)

3 tablespoons melted coconut oil

zest of 1 lemon, plus 1 tablespoon lemon juice

1 tablespoon chopped thyme

2 tablespoons chopped dill

2 tablespoons chopped chives

sea salt and freshly ground black pepper, to taste

See image, page 97, rear

1 Preheat the oven to 200°C (400°F). Peel the sweet potatoes and apples and cut into 5 cm (2-inch) pieces. Slice the mini potatoes in half.

2 In a large bowl, toss the potatoes and apple with coconut oil, lemon zest and juice. Spread out on a baking sheet or in a large roasting tin and sprinkle with salt, pepper and thyme. Bake for 45 minutes, stirring every 15 minutes, until cooked through and golden brown.

3 Remove from the oven, transfer to a serving bowl, toss with the dill and chives, and serve.

CALORIES (PER SERVING)	170
PROTEIN	2.1 G
TOTAL FAT	7.1 G
SATURATED FAT	5.9 G
CARBOHYDRATES	26.6 G
DIETARY FIBRE	4.1 G
SUGARS	8.6 G
VITAMINS	A, B6, C

PEPITA PESTO-STUFFED MUSHROOM CAPS

Serves 4–6
gluten-free

Who doesn't like stuffed mushrooms? Especially those filled with a spinach and pumpkin seed pesto that's rich in zinc for immune support.

Prep: 15 mins | Cook: 10 mins

18–20 cremini mushrooms
a little oil, for brushing
1 tablespoon nutritional yeast

FOR THE PESTO
60 g (2 oz) baby spinach
25 g (¾ oz) basil
140 g (4¾ oz) pumpkin seeds
60 ml (2 fl oz) extra-virgin olive oil
2 garlic cloves
juice of ½ lemon
1 teaspoon sea salt
freshly ground black pepper,
to taste
See image, page 97, front left

1 Preheat a grill to medium. Clean the mushrooms gently and snap off the stems. Brush the caps with oil and place stem-side up on a baking sheet. Place under the preheated grill for 4 to 5 minutes, until lightly browned and the juices have released. Flip and cook for another 2 minutes. Remove from the grill.

2 For the pesto, combine the ingredients in a food processor and process to a smooth paste, stopping to scrape down the sides as necessary.

3 Spoon 1 or 2 teaspoons of pesto into each mushroom cap, depending on size, mounding it up. Any leftover pesto can be stored, covered, in the fridge for up to 1 week, or frozen for later use. Sprinkle with nutritional yeast and place under the grill for another 2 to 3 minutes, until sizzling. Serve hot from the oven.

SUPERFOOD TIP: Up the omegas by using flax or hemp oil in the pesto in place of olive oil.

CALORIES (PER SERVING)	226
PROTEIN	7.6 G
TOTAL FAT	20.5 G
SATURATED FAT	3.4 G
CARBOHYDRATES	6.6 G
DIETARY FIBRE	1.7 G
SUGARS	0.7 G
VITAMINS	B6

BRUSSELS SPROUT LATKES WITH TOFU 'SOUR CREAM'

Serves 4–6
gluten-free
option

Here's one of several Brussels sprout recipes in the book that promise to make fans out of sceptics. So much phytochemical goodness is hiding in these crispy little patties! For a gluten-free option, use gluten-free flour in place of plain flour.

Prep: 15 mins | Cook: 15 mins

180 g (6¼ oz) shredded Brussels sprouts
½ onion, thinly sliced
1 medium potato, grated
2 chia eggs (page 17)
30 g (1 oz) plain flour
pinch of paprika
sea salt and freshly ground black pepper, to taste
a little oil, for frying
chopped chives, to serve

FOR THE TOFU 'SOUR CREAM'
1 x 350 g (12 oz) package silken tofu
2 tablespoons umeboshi vinegar
1 tablespoon extra-virgin olive oil
1 tablespoon water
½ teaspoon chopped fresh dill, or ¼ teaspoon dried dill
¼ teaspoon sea salt

See image, opposite, right

1 In a medium bowl, mix together the Brussels sprouts, onion and potato. Add the chia eggs and toss to combine.

2 In a small bowl, stir together the flour, paprika and a little sea salt and pepper. Sprinkle this over the vegetable mixture and fold in to create a thick batter.

3 Heat a little oil in a frying pan over a high heat. Scoop out 60 ml (2 fl oz) of batter and place in the oil, flattening it with the back of a spatula. Repeat with three more scoops to fill the pan. Cook for 2 to 3 minutes, until golden brown, then flip and cook for an additional 2 to 3 minutes until the underside is also golden brown. Remove to a plate lined with paper towels and then repeat with the remaining batter. If not serving immediately, keep warm in the oven at 120°C (250°F).

4 For the tofu 'sour cream', place all the ingredients in a blender or food processor and blend until smooth. Alternatively, a hand-held immersion blender can be used. Any leftover cream can be stored for up to five days in the fridge.

5 To serve, top the latkes with a dollop of cream and a sprinkle of chives.

CALORIES (PER SERVING)	129
PROTEIN	7.5 G
TOTAL FAT	5.9 G
SATURATED FAT	1.0 G
CARBOHYDRATES	14.3 G
DIETARY FIBRE	3.4 G
SUGARS	1.6 G
VITAMINS	C

CRISPY ROASTED BRUSSELS SPROUTS WITH FRESH HERBS

Serves 4
gluten-free

This is one of those recipes that I almost feel silly putting in the book because it's such as classic, but I just had to include it for those of you who have yet to discover the magic of roasted Brussels sprouts.

Prep: 10 mins | Cook: 30 mins

450 g (1 lb) Brussels sprouts

1 tablespoon melted coconut oil

sea salt and freshly ground black pepper, to taste

2 tablespoons chopped dill, parsley or basil

See image, page 100, left

1 Preheat the oven to 190°C (375°F). Line a baking sheet with baking paper.

2 Trim the outer leaves of the Brussels sprouts and cut the sprouts in half. If some are significantly larger they can be quartered to ensure even cooking.

3 In a large bowl, toss the sprouts in the oil and season lightly. Transfer them to the baking sheet and bake for 25 to 30 minutes, flipping halfway, until golden brown and the edges have begun to crisp. Remove from the oven and toss with the fresh herbs and a final pinch of sea salt.

CALORIES (PER SERVING)	78
PROTEIN	3.8 G
TOTAL FAT	3.8 G
SATURATED FAT	3.1 G
CARBOHYDRATES	10.2 G
DIETARY FIBRE	4.2 G
SUGARS	2.4 G
VITAMINS	A, C

COCONUT LEMONGRASS RICE

Serves 4–6
gluten-free

This rice has a wonderful flavour of coconut and fragrant lemongrass and is a beautifully easy side dish. It is a great recipe to use when entertaining a crowd; if you're cooking for two, you can halve the quantities with the same delicious results.

Prep: 5 mins | Cook: 30 mins

500 ml (18 fl oz) water

250 ml (9 fl oz) coconut milk

360 g (12½ oz) basmati or jasmine rice

2 stalks lemongrass

40 g (1½ oz), plus 1 tablespoon unsweetened desiccated coconut

1 teaspoon sea salt

½ teaspoon chilli flakes (optional)

See image, page 140, rear

1 Place the water, coconut milk and rice in a large pot and bring to a boil. While this is coming to a boil, chop the lemongrass stalks into 10-cm (4-inch) pieces and bruise them by scoring with a knife.

2 Add 40 g (1½ oz) of desiccated coconut, the lemongrass and salt to the pot; cover, reduce heat to low, and simmer for 25 minutes until the water has been absorbed and the rice is tender.

3 Top the cooked rice with the remaining coconut and chilli flakes, if using, and serve.

CALORIES (PER SERVING)	354
PROTEIN	5.6 G
TOTAL FAT	15.6 G
SATURATED FAT	13.2 G
CARBOHYDRATES	49.8 G
DIETARY FIBRE	3.5 G
SUGARS	2.0 G
VITAMINS	C

MAIN MEALS

TEMPEH BRASSICA BIBIMBAP

Serves 2–3
gluten-free

Cabbage, broccoli, daikon and Brussels sprouts top this rice bowl, inspired by the Korean dish. High in vitamins A, C and K, with a multitude of antioxidants and anti-inflammatory properties, they make this meal a real superfood feast.

Prep: 15 mins | Cook: 30 mins

110 g (4 oz) tempeh
2 tablespoons coconut oil
10 Brussels sprouts, halved
90 g (3¼ oz) broccoli florets
570 g (1 lb 4 oz) cooked short-grain brown rice
1 carrot, julienned
150 g (5 oz) julienned daikon
40 g (1½ oz) finely shredded green cabbage
40 g (1½ oz) finely shredded red cabbage
2 teaspoons toasted sesame seeds
1 spring onion, thinly sliced
1 tablespoon hot chilli sauce
sea salt, to taste

FOR THE SAUCE

2 tablespoons toasted sesame oil
2 tablespoons rice vinegar
1 tablespoon brown sugar
½ tablespoon minced fresh ginger

See image, opposite, front

1 Steam the tempeh for 15 minutes. Slice into 0.3-cm (⅛-inch) thick pieces and set aside.

2 Heat 1 tablespoon of coconut oil in a frying pan and add the tempeh. Sprinkle with sea salt and cook for 5 minutes per side, until golden brown. Remove to a plate.

3 Add ½ tablespoon of coconut oil to the frying pan, followed by the Brussels sprouts, cooking for 5 minutes per side, until golden brown. Remove to a bowl.

4 Heat the remaining oil in the frying pan and add the broccoli, cooking for about 6 minutes, stirring often, until cooked but still a little crunchy. Add to the bowl with the Brussels sprouts.

5 To make the sauce, whisk all the ingredients in a bowl.

6 To serve, divide the rice between individual serving bowls. Arrange the tempeh, Brussels sprouts, broccoli, carrot, daikon and cabbages on top, then top with sauce and sprinkle with sesame seeds, spring onion and a dollop of hot sauce.

CALORIES (PER SERVING)	483
PROTEIN	15.8 G
TOTAL FAT	24.6 G
SATURATED FAT	10.2 G
CARBOHYDRATES	55.9 G
DIETARY FIBRE	7.8 G
SUGARS	9.1 G
VITAMINS	C

WILD RICE AND KALE WELLNESS BOWL

One-bowl meals are a favourite of mine — satisfying and filling, but full of nutritious grains and vegetables. This bowl boasts a vitamin-rich combination of kale, goji berries, pumpkin and sunflower seeds, with a delicious creamy sauce.

Prep: 15 mins | Cook: 45 mins

180 g (6¼ oz) wild rice

1 x 400 ml (14 oz) tin adzuki beans, drained and rinsed

4 kale leaves

1 teaspoon extra-virgin olive oil

pinch of sea salt

1 tomato, diced

125 ml (4½ fl oz) Creamy Matcha Dressing (page 50)

35 g (1¼ oz) sunflower seeds

35 g (1¼ oz) pumpkin seeds

2 tablespoons goji berries

See image, page 107, rear

1 Cook the rice according to the packet instructions. Fluff with a fork and leave uncovered to cool for 5 to 10 minutes then fold in the adzuki beans.

2 Wash and dry the kale leaves. Remove the tough stems (page 17) and finely slice the leaves. In a large bowl, massage the kale with the olive oil and salt.

3 Divide the rice and bean mixture, kale, and tomato into two serving bowls along with half the dressing and toss. Top with the seeds, berries and remaining dressing, and serve.

CALORIES (PER SERVING)	799
PROTEIN	35.2 G
TOTAL FAT	19.0 G
SATURATED FAT	2.9 G
CARBOHYDRATES	133.3 G
DIETARY FIBRE	23.6 G
SUGARS	10.9 G
VITAMINS	A, C

BLACK BEAN HEMP PATTIES

Serves 4
gluten-free

Shelled hemp seeds and black beans make for nutty, pan-fried patties that are perfect on top of a green salad, wrapped in a collard green or served on a bun as a traditional burger.

Prep: 20 mins (plus up to 6 hrs' chilling) | Cook: 20 mins

1 x 425 g (15 oz) tin black beans, drained and rinsed

1 large carrot, grated

4 spring onions, sliced

75 g (2½ oz) shelled hemp seeds

190 g (6¾ oz) cooked brown rice

1 tablespoon liquid aminos or gluten-free tamari

2 teaspoons apple cider vinegar

½ teaspoon smoked paprika

½ teaspoon sea salt

¼ teaspoon freshly ground black pepper

1 tablespoon coconut oil

See image, page 111, rear

1 Place the beans, carrot, onions, hemp seeds, rice, aminos, vinegar, paprika, salt and pepper in a food processor and pulse to combine. Continue pulsing until some of the beans and rice have been broken down, but still many remain whole. Refrigerate the mixture for at least 30 minutes, or up to 6 hours.

2 Form the mixture into four patties (or eight if you prefer smaller, crispier patties). Heat the oil in a frying pan over a medium-high heat. Add the patties and cook for 4 to 5 minutes per side, until crispy and heated through.

CALORIES (PER SERVING)	335
PROTEIN	17.0 G
TOTAL FAT	13.2 G
SATURATED FAT	3.5 G
CARBOHYDRATES	43.2 G
DIETARY FIBRE	10.9 G
SUGARS	2.4 G
VITAMINS	A

SUNDRIED TOMATO AND COCONUT QUINOA BURGERS

Coconut and sundried tomatoes are amazing together, and combined with super-seed quinoa, these burgers are top-notch. For a gluten-free option, use gluten-free buns.

Prep: 25 mins | Cook: 30 mins

85 g (3 oz) quinoa (or 190 g/6¾ oz) leftover cooked quinoa)

375 ml (13 fl oz) water

8–10 sundried tomatoes (dry-packed, not in oil)

25 g (¾ oz) unsweetened desiccated coconut

1 garlic clove, minced

2 tablespoons pumpkin purée (page 17) or tinned pumpkin

1 tablespoon melted coconut oil, plus extra for cooking

2 teaspoons fennel seeds

4 burger buns

sea salt and freshly ground black pepper, to taste

salad greens, sprouts, avocado, to serve

See image, opposite, front

1 Rinse the quinoa in a fine mesh sieve. In a small pan, bring the quinoa and water to a boil over a medium heat. Reduce the heat to low, cover, and simmer for 15 minutes, or until the liquid has been absorbed. Remove from the heat and leave, covered, for an additional 5 minutes. Fluff with a fork and set aside.

2 Rehydrate the tomatoes in a bowl of hot water for 10 minutes. Drain, reserving the soaking liquid.

3 Combine the quinoa, tomatoes, coconut, garlic, pumpkin, 1 tablespoon coconut oil and fennel seeds in a food processor and pulse until the mixture comes together enough to be able to form patties and have them hold together. Add a splash or two of the tomato soaking water if necessary to help bind the ingredients. Season to taste.

4 Form the mixture into four patties. Heat a little coconut oil in a frying pan over a medium-high heat and cook each patty for 5 minutes per side, until crispy on the outside and warmed through. They are a little on the delicate side, so take care when flipping them that they don't break apart. Serve on burger buns with tender salad greens or sprouts and a wedge of avocado.

VARIATION: For an oil-free option, the burgers can be baked in the oven at 180°C (350°F) for 20 minutes.

CALORIES (PER SERVING)	293
PROTEIN	8.6 G
TOTAL FAT	10.0 G
SATURATED FAT	6.0 G
CARBOHYDRATES	44.7 G
DIETARY FIBRE	4.6 G
SUGARS	8.7 G
VITAMINS	A

SWEET POTATO MAC 'N' CHEESE

The thyroid-supporting superfood sweet potato takes centre stage in this rich and creamy mac 'n' cheese, providing both the base and vibrant colour. For a gluten-free option, choose a quinoa or brown rice pasta.

Prep: 15 mins | Cook: 30 mins

340 g (12 oz) short-cut whole-wheat pasta (elbows, mini shells, bowties, penne, etc.)
260 g (9¼ oz) chopped sweet potato
100 g (3½ oz) chopped cauliflower
1 shallot
1 garlic clove
375 ml (13 fl oz) unsweetened non-dairy milk (of choice)
½ tablespoon Dijon mustard
2 tablespoons miso paste
15 g (½ oz) nutritional yeast
1½ teaspoons sea salt
1 teaspoon lemon juice
¼ teaspoon chilli flakes

FOR THE HEMP 'PARMESAN'

15 g (½ oz) nutritional yeast
75 g (2½ oz) shelled hemp seeds
1 teaspoon sea salt
¼ teaspoon garlic powder (optional)

1 Preheat the oven to 190°C (375°F).

2 In a large pot, cook the pasta until al dente, about 1 to 2 minutes less than advised on the packet. Drain and set aside.

3 Steam the sweet potato, cauliflower, shallot and garlic for 8 to 10 minutes, or until the sweet potatoes are very soft. Place in a blender with all the remaining ingredients and blend until smooth. Taste and adjust the seasonings to suit.

4 To make the hemp 'parmesan', combine all the ingredients in a food processor and pulse to combine.

5 Pour the pasta into a lightly oiled 23 x 33-cm (9 x 13-inch) baking dish, cover with the sauce, and stir well to coat the pasta with sauce. Sprinkle a quarter of the hemp parmesan on top, cover with foil, and bake for 20 minutes, until the pasta is tender and heated through. Remove the foil and bake for another 5 minutes to brown the top. Serve with an extra sprinkling of hemp parmesan if desired. The remaining parmesan will keep for at least two weeks in a sealed container in the fridge.

CALORIES (PER SERVING)	344
PROTEIN	15.4 G
TOTAL FAT	9.4 G
SATURATED FAT	0.7 G
CARBOHYDRATES	51.7 G
DIETARY FIBRE	9.9 G
SUGARS	6.3 G
VITAMINS	A, B6

GNOCCHI WITH ROASTED GARLIC AND KALE PURÉE

Roasted garlic makes this dish shine with its mellow, creamy, antibacterial goodness. Shop-bought gnocchi is readily available and really quite good, and if you already have roasted garlic on hand (see tip), this amazing superfood pasta is an easy weeknight meal to throw together.

Prep: 10 mins | Cook: 60 mins

1 garlic head

60 ml (2 fl oz) olive oil

280 g (10 oz) kale leaves, woody stems removed (page 17)

2 tablespoons lemon juice

450 g (1 lb) gnocchi

150 g (5 oz) halved red and yellow cherry tomatoes

sea salt and freshly ground black pepper, to taste

See image, opposite, front

1 Preheat the oven to 200°C (400°F). Slice the top off the head of garlic, exposing the cloves. Place in the middle of a piece of aluminium foil and drizzle ½ tablespoon of olive oil over the top. Wrap the foil around it into a little package and place in a baking dish. Bake for 45 minutes, or until the cloves are soft and pierce easily with a knife. Set aside to cool down enough to work with.

2 Place the kale leaves, remaining olive oil and lemon juice into a food processor. From the base of the head, gently squeeze the garlic until all of the soft, caramelised cloves pop out into the bowl of the food processor. Process until smooth, stopping to scrape down the sides as you go. Season to taste.

3 In a large pot, cook the gnocchi according to the packet instructions, then drain, reserving 250 ml (9 fl oz) of the cooking water. Return the gnocchi to the pot and add the kale purée, along with as much reserved water as needed to thin the sauce to your taste. Cook over a medium heat just long enough to heat the sauce through. Fold in the tomatoes and serve.

SUPERFOOD TIP: Roasted garlic is so creamy and delicious that it can be spread directly onto crostini. When taking the time to roast garlic, it's worth baking a few extra heads at the same time for later use. The garlic can be stored in the fridge in an airtight container for up to a week.

CALORIES (PER SERVING)	353
PROTEIN	10.4 G
TOTAL FAT	14.8 G
SATURATED FAT	2.1 G
CARBOHYDRATES	46.9 G
DIETARY FIBRE	1.5 G
SUGARS	1.1 G
VITAMINS	A, C

ITALIAN-STYLE PUMPKIN RISOTTO

Serves 4–6
gluten-free

Creamy risotto is a rich addition to any dinner table, and an impressive meal to serve to guests. The pumpkin shines and gives this dish a wonderful orange hue.

Prep: 5 mins | Cook: 40 mins

1.25 litres (39½ fl oz) vegetable broth

2 tablespoons coconut oil

1 onion, minced

2 garlic cloves, minced

360 g (12½ oz) arborio rice

190 ml (6½ fl oz) white wine

330 g (11½ oz) pumpkin purée (page 17) or tinned pumpkin (not pumpkin pie filling)

sea salt and freshly ground black pepper, to taste

pinch of nutmeg

See image, page 115, rear

1 In a small pot, heat the vegetable broth over a low heat – it should be hot when it's added to the rice.

2 Heat the oil in a large pan over a medium heat. Add the onion and sauté for 5 minutes, then add the garlic and stir continuously for 1 minute. Next, add the dry rice and stir to coat it with the oil. Cook for another 2 minutes.

3 Add the wine to the rice and stir until it has all been absorbed. Add 250 ml (9 fl oz) of the broth and keep stirring as the rice cooks and this too is absorbed. Repeat for each additional 250 ml (9 fl oz) of broth, adding more as the previous batch has cooked down. This will take about 20 minutes of cooking and stirring. After the fourth addition of broth has been cooked down, taste the risotto to see if the rice is cooked through; if not, add the remaining broth.

4 Once the rice is cooked, fold in the pumpkin purée, increase the heat, and cook for around 2 to 3 minutes until heated through. Season to taste with salt, pepper and a pinch of nutmeg, and serve.

CALORIES (PER SERVING)	255
PROTEIN	3.9 G
TOTAL FAT	4.7 G
SATURATED FAT	4.0 G
CARBOHYDRATES	44.9 G
DIETARY FIBRE	2.9 G
SUGARS	4.5 G
VITAMINS	A

PENNE WITH LENTILS, OLIVES AND KALE

Serves 4
gluten-free
option

Filling lentils, briny olives, gorgeous green kale and caramelised onions – what's not to like? With only a handful of ingredients this is a hearty, heart-healthy meal that's an easy fix. For a gluten-free option, use gluten-free pasta.

Prep: 5 mins | Cook: 40 mins

100 g (3½ oz) French or puy lentils, rinsed
375 ml (13 fl oz) water
3 tablespoons extra-virgin olive oil
1 onion, halved and finely sliced
225 g (8 oz) whole-wheat penne
225 g (8 oz) kale leaves
10 green olives, pitted and chopped
pinch of chilli flakes
sea salt and freshly ground black pepper, to taste

See image, page 119, rear

1 In a large pan, bring the lentils and water to a boil over a medium heat. Reduce the heat to low and cook for 30 to 35 minutes, until tender. Drain and set aside until the pasta is cooked.

2 Heat 1 tablespoon of oil in a large frying pan and add the onion. Cook over a medium heat for 15 minutes, stirring every few minutes, until the onions have begun to caramelise.

3 Cook the pasta according to the packet instructions, until about 2 minutes shy of al dente. Wash and dry the kale leaves. Remove the tough stems (page 17) and finely slice the leaves. Add the kale to the cooking water and cook for another 2 minutes. Drain, reserving 125 ml (4½ fl oz) of the cooking water.

4 Add the pasta and kale to the onion pan along with the lentils, olives, the remaining olive oil and chilli flakes. Increase the heat to high and sizzle for 30 seconds, adding a little of the reserved cooking water if needed, to keep it moist. Season to taste with salt and pepper, and serve.

CALORIES (PER SERVING)	410
PROTEIN	14.5 G
TOTAL FAT	13.6 G
SATURATED FAT	1.8 G
CARBOHYDRATES	59.1 G
DIETARY FIBRE	11.0 G
SUGARS	2.8 G
VITAMINS	A, C

SPAGHETTI AND QUINOA 'MEATBALLS'

Serves 4–6
gluten-free
option

A big ol' bowl of spaghetti and 'meatballs', created by mixing quinoa and vegetables in a flavourful blend. For a gluten-free option, use gluten-free spaghetti.

Prep: 20 mins | Cook: 20 mins

2 tablespoons extra-virgin olive oil

2 shallots, minced

60 ml (2 fl oz) white wine

1 teaspoon lemon juice

1 x 800 g (28 oz) tin diced tomatoes, puréed

225 g (8 oz) uncooked spaghetti

chopped parsley and basil, to serve

sea salt and freshly ground black pepper, to taste

FOR THE 'MEATBALLS'

85 g (3 oz) quinoa

250 ml (9 fl oz) vegetable broth

5 cremini mushrooms, diced

1 small celery stalk, diced

25 g (¾ oz) kale leaves, woody stems removed (page 17), chopped

1 tablespoon tomato paste

2 teaspoons liquid aminos or gluten-free tamari

1 teaspoon vegan Worcestershire sauce (optional)

See image, opposite, front

CALORIES (PER SERVING)	276
PROTEIN	8.4 G
TOTAL FAT	6.1 G
SATURATED FAT	0.9 G
CARBOHYDRATES	78.0 G
DIETARY FIBRE	3.5 G
SUGARS	4.8 G
VITAMINS	A, C

1 For the 'meatballs', rinse the quinoa well in a fine mesh sieve. In a small pan, bring the quinoa and broth to a boil over a medium heat. Reduce the heat to low, cover, and simmer for 15 minutes, or until all the liquid has been absorbed. Remove from the heat and leave, covered, for an additional 5 minutes. Fluff with a fork and set aside.

2 Preheat the oven to 190°C (375°F). Line a baking sheet with baking paper.

3 Place the cooked quinoa with the remaining meatball ingredients and a little ground black pepper in a food processor and pulse until combined, but still with some texture (don't reduce it to a paste). Scoop out 1 tablespoon at a time, rolling it into a ball and placing on the lined sheet. Once all the balls have been rolled, spritz with a little oil and bake for 15 minutes, until lightly browned and cooked through.

4 Heat the oil in a pan over a medium-high heat and sauté the shallots for 2 to 3 minutes, until softened. Add the white wine, lemon juice and puréed tomatoes and simmer, partially covered, for 15 to 20 minutes, stirring occasionally, until the sauce thickens slightly. Season to taste.

5 While the sauce is cooking, bring a large pot of salted water to a boil. Cook the pasta according to the packet instructions until al dente, about 7 to 10 minutes. Drain and add to the sauce along with half the baked quinoa balls and fold together. Place in a serving dish and top with the remaining meatballs and the herbs.

MEDITERRANEAN AMARANTH PIZZA

Serves 2–4
gluten-free

This amaranth pizza crust has a really crispy texture, yet is still a little chewy in the middle. Topped with creamy beans, tangy olives and artichokes, it's better than any run-of-the-mill takeaway.

Prep: 15 mins | Cook: 30 mins

190 g (6¾ oz) amaranth, soaked for 8 hours
170 g (5¾ oz) quinoa flakes
60 ml (2 fl oz) water
1½ teaspoons baking powder
2 tablespoons melted coconut oil
170 g (5¾ oz) cooked white beans (Great Northern, cannellini or white kidney beans)
2 roasted garlic cloves (page 114)
1 tablespoon extra-virgin olive oil
½ teaspoon rosemary
35 g (1¼ oz) chopped black olives
85 g (3 oz) chopped artichoke hearts
85 g (3 oz) micro greens, rocket or sprouts
sea salt and freshly ground black pepper, to taste

See image, page 104

1 Preheat the oven to 230°C (450°F).

2 To make the crust, drain the soaked amaranth and rinse with clean water, using a nut milk bag or fine mesh sieve lined with cheesecloth, otherwise the amaranth will sneak right through your sieve. Place the drained amaranth in a food processor with the quinoa flakes, water, baking powder and ½ teaspoon of salt, and blend until almost smooth.

3 Place a 25-cm (10-inch) oven safe frying pan in the oven to preheat for 5 minutes. With great care, remove the pan and oil the bottom with the coconut oil, then add the amaranth purée, spreading it out evenly almost to the edges using a silicone spatula. Bake for 12 to 15 minutes, until the edges are lightly browned and it's firm enough to get a sturdy metal spatula underneath and lift. Gently loosen the entire crust with the metal spatula and, with care, flip and bake for another 10 minutes.

4 While the crust is cooking, combine the beans, garlic, olive oil and rosemary in a food processor and blend until smooth. Season to taste.

5 Spread the bean purée over the top of the cooked pizza crust and top with the olives and artichoke hearts. Return to the oven for 5 minutes to heat the toppings through. Remove, top with micro greens, slice, and serve.

CALORIES (PER SERVING)	470
PROTEIN	16.3 G
TOTAL FAT	15.3 G
SATURATED FAT	7.7 G
CARBOHYDRATES	69.4 G
DIETARY FIBRE	13.8 G
SUGARS	1.8 G
VITAMINS	B1, B6, C

ORANGE-GLAZED CARROTS WITH DILL QUINOA

Serves 4
gluten-free

I like to enjoy this meal in the summer using locally farmed carrots, packed with beta-carotene, which is essential for skin, eye and immune health. I love how the sweetness of the orange juice and the fresh taste of the dill quinoa combine to make a beautiful seasonal dish.

Prep: 10 mins | Cook: 25 mins

170 g (5¾ oz) quinoa
500 ml (18 fl oz) water
2 bunches slim carrots
1 tablespoon coconut oil
zest of 1 orange
250 ml (9 fl oz) orange juice
2 tablespoons minced fresh ginger
1 head Bibb lettuce
2 tablespoons chopped dill
1 tablespoon chopped parsley
sea salt and freshly ground black pepper, to taste

See image, page 123, rear

1 Rinse the quinoa well in a fine mesh sieve. In a small pan, bring the quinoa, water and ½ teaspoon of sea salt to a boil over a medium heat. Reduce the heat to low, cover, and simmer for 15 minutes, or until all the liquid has been absorbed. Remove from the heat and leave, covered, for an additional 5 minutes. Fluff with a fork and set aside in a serving dish.

2 Meanwhile, bring a pot of water, large enough to fit the carrots, to a boil, and parboil the carrots for 5 to 6 minutes, then drain.

3 In a separate pan, heat the oil over a medium-high heat, then add the zest, orange juice and ginger, and bring to a boil. Add the carrots, reduce the heat to low, and simmer until the liquid has reduced by half, about 3 to 4 minutes. Season to taste.

4 Tear the lettuce into bite-sized pieces and fold into the quinoa with the dill. Top with the glazed carrots, sprinkle with the parsley, and serve.

CALORIES (PER SERVING)	313
PROTEIN	8.6 G
TOTAL FAT	6.4 G
SATURATED FAT	3.3 G
CARBOHYDRATES	56.9 G
DIETARY FIBRE	8.6 G
SUGARS	15.6 G
VITAMINS	A, B6, C

HEMP-CRUSTED TOFU WITH
GARLIC-CHILLI COLLARDS

Serves 4
gluten-free

This tofu reminds me a little of that retro shake 'n' bake breading mix, except this one is based around shelled hemp seeds, nutritional yeast and herbs. My toddler gobbles these up!

Prep: 15 mins | Cook: 20 mins

1 x 350 g (12 oz) packet firm or extra-firm tofu

2 tablespoons apple cider vinegar

2 tablespoons liquid aminos or gluten-free tamari

2 tablespoons coconut oil

35 g (1¼ oz) shelled hemp seeds

2 tablespoons polenta

2 tablespoons nutritional yeast

½ teaspoon dried basil

½ teaspoon dried oregano

½ teaspoon dried thyme

1 bunch collard greens

2 garlic cloves, minced

pinch of chilli flakes

2 tablespoons white wine or vegetable broth

sea salt and freshly ground black pepper, to taste

See image, opposite, front

1 To prepare the tofu, wrap it in a clean tea towel and gently press the water out of it, either by hand or by placing it on a plate and weighing it down with a cast-iron pan or a few books. After 15 minutes cut it into eight slices, then cut each rectangle into triangles and place in a shallow dish. Cover with the vinegar and liquid aminos and leave to marinate for 10 minutes.

2 Heat 1 tablespoon of the coconut oil in a large pan over a medium-high heat. In a large bowl, combine the hemp seeds, polenta, nutritional yeast, basil, oregano, thyme and 1 teaspoon of sea salt. Coat each piece of tofu in this mixture and place in the pan. Cook for 5 to 6 minutes, then flip over and cook for another 5 minutes, until both sides are lightly browned.

3 While the tofu is cooking, wash the collard leaves, remove the tough middle stem from each leaf and discard. Stack the leaves and chop into large, bite-sized pieces. Heat the remaining coconut oil in another pan over a medium heat and add the garlic and chilli flakes, cooking for 3 to 4 minutes, until fragrant but not browning. Add the collard greens and wine or broth and cook for 8 to 10 minutes, until the greens are tender. Season to taste with salt and pepper and serve alongside the hemp-crusted tofu.

VARIATION: If you can't find collards, use kale as your chosen green.

CALORIES (PER SERVING)	217
PROTEIN	13.8 G
TOTAL FAT	15.8 G
SATURATED FAT	6.9 G
CARBOHYDRATES	59.2 G
DIETARY FIBRE	3.8 G
SUGARS	0.7 G
VITAMINS	B6, B12

CHILLI-RUBBED
SWEET POTATO TOSTADAS

Serves 2–3
gluten-free

I never get sick of Mexican fare, but when I do reach my fill of tacos, I like to bake the tortillas into crunchy tostadas that are served like mini open sandwiches. They're not easy to eat, so be prepared for a little mess!

Prep: 20 mins | Cook: 30 mins

FOR THE SWEET POTATOES

1 large or 2 medium sweet potatoes, peeled and cut into 1.25-cm (½-inch) cubes

2 teaspoons chilli powder

½ teaspoon dried oregano

½ teaspoon garlic powder

¼ teaspoon smoked paprika

1 tablespoon lime juice

FOR THE SALSA

85 g (3 oz) cooked black beans (drained and rinsed if using tinned)

1 tomato, diced

40 g (1½ oz) diced white or red onion

5 g (⅛ oz) coriander, chopped

juice of ½ lime

pinch of sea salt

FOR THE CREMA

1 avocado

½ spring onion

60 ml (2 fl oz) plain non-dairy yogurt or silken tofu

2 teaspoons lime juice

½ teaspoon sea salt

3 tablespoons water

FOR THE TOSTADAS

6 corn tortillas (or use shop-bought tostada shells)

oil, for brushing

See image, opposite, front

1 Preheat the oven to 220°C (425°F). Line a baking sheet with baking paper.

2 For the sweet potatoes, place the potato cubes in a large pot of boiling water and parboil for 3 minutes. Drain and spread out on a tea towel to dry. Transfer the potato to a large bowl and toss with the chilli powder, oregano, garlic powder, paprika and lime juice. Place on the baking sheet and bake for 15 minutes. Remove from the oven and reduce the heat to 180°C (350°F).

3 Make the salsa by combining the beans, tomato, onion, coriander, lime juice and a pinch of sea salt in a bowl.

4 For the crema, combine the avocado, onion, yogurt, lime juice, salt and water in a blender or food processor and process until smooth. Season to taste with more salt or lime, if desired.

5 To make the tostadas, brush each tortilla lightly with oil and bake on a baking sheet in the oven for 4 to 5 minutes each side, until crunchy. They'll continue to firm up as they cool.

6 To assemble, top each crispy tortilla with a little salsa, followed by the sweet potato, and top with a dollop of avocado crema.

CALORIES (PER SERVING)	374
PROTEIN	9.3 G
TOTAL FAT	16.9 G
SATURATED FAT	3.5 G
CARBOHYDRATES	50.9 G
DIETARY FIBRE	13.5 G
SUGARS	5.7 G
VITAMINS	A

CACAO MOLE TOFU WITH SLAW

Serves 4
gluten-free

There are many varieties of mole, a traditional Mexican sauce that features dried chillies, nuts, seeds, spices, dried fruit and even chocolate. This is my superfood twist on a chocolate mole, using antioxidant-rich cacao instead.

Prep: 15 mins | Cook: 40 mins

4 dried ancho chillies

2 tablespoons coconut oil

1 onion, diced

4 garlic cloves, minced

225 g (8 oz) puréed tomatoes

40g (1½ oz) almonds

3 tablespoons pumpkin seeds

1 tablespoon raisins (optional)

3 tablespoons cacao powder

1 teaspoon cinnamon

1 teaspoon cumin seeds

1 teaspoon dried oregano

½ teaspoon smoked paprika

up to 500 ml (18 fl oz) vegetable broth

1 x Hemp-crusted Tofu (page 122)

1 teaspoon sea salt

toasted sesame seeds, to serve

FOR THE SLAW

½ head green cabbage, finely shredded

2 carrots, grated

¼ mild onion, finely sliced

10 g (¼ oz) coriander, chopped

1 tablespoon white balsamic vinegar

pinch of sea salt

See image, page 124, rear, left

1 For the slaw, combine all the ingredients in a large bowl and mix well. Set aside.

2 Soak the dried chillies in hot water for 15 to 20 minutes until softened. Drain and set aside.

3 In a large pan, heat the oil over a medium-high heat. Add the onion and garlic and sauté for 5 minutes, then add the tomatoes, almonds, pumpkin seeds, raisins, if using, and softened chillies. Reduce the heat to medium and cook for another 10 minutes. Add the cacao powder, spices, 1 teaspoon of sea salt and 250 ml (9 fl oz) of broth, and simmer for 15 minutes.

4 Remove from the heat, leave to cool for 10 minutes, then place in a blender and blend until smooth. Return to the pan to reheat; an additional 125–250 ml (4½–9 fl oz) of broth can be added to the sauce to thin it if desired. Season to taste with salt.

5 Make the Hemp-crusted Tofu (page 122). Spoon the heated sauce over the tofu, sprinkle with toasted sesame seeds, and serve alongside the slaw. Any leftover mole sauce can be stored in the fridge for up to four days, or frozen for later use; it's great over potatoes or as a burrito filling.

CALORIES (PER SERVING)	400
PROTEIN	18.3 G
TOTAL FAT	26.5 G
SATURATED FAT	13.9 G
CARBOHYDRATES	79.1 G
DIETARY FIBRE	8.0 G
SUGARS	11.7 G
VITAMINS	A, B6, B12

SUNFLOWER SEED, PINEAPPLE AND CHICKPEA TACOS

Serves 4–6
gluten-free

Superfood turmeric makes this taco filling vibrant in colour, and juicy pineapple makes it sing with flavour. Perfect for an outdoor meal on a sunny day, or even the coldest day when you want to dream of warmer times.

Prep: 10 mins | Cook: 20 mins

1 tablespoon extra-virgin olive oil

½ red onion, sliced into half-moons

1 x 425 g (15 oz) tin chickpeas, drained and rinsed

165 g (5½ oz) diced pineapple

75 g (2½ oz) sunflower seeds

1 teaspoon ground cumin

2 teaspoons turmeric

½ teaspoon sea salt

12 fresh corn tortillas

90 g (3¼ oz) shredded lettuce

2 radishes, thinly sliced

fresh coriander leaves, torn

1 x Tofu 'Sour Cream' (page 101)

See image, page 124, rear, right

1 Heat the oil in a frying pan over a medium-high heat, add the onions, and sauté for 4 to 5 minutes. Add the chickpeas, pineapple, sunflower seeds, spices and salt, and cook for 10 minutes, until warmed through and the flavours combined.

2 Warm the tortillas in another lightly oiled frying pan, about 30 seconds per side, until soft and pliable. Use a large pan, if possible, so that you can heat two or three at a time.

3 To serve, fill each tortilla with a little of the cooked filling, and top with lettuce, radishes, coriander and the tofu 'sour cream'.

CALORIES (PER SERVING)	359
PROTEIN	15.4 G
TOTAL FAT	16.6 G
SATURATED FAT	2.1 G
CARBOHYDRATES	41.1 G
DIETARY FIBRE	8.1 G
SUGARS	4.6 G
VITAMINS	B6

ROASTED ROOT VEGETABLE AND CURRIED BARLEY BOWL

Serves 4
gluten-free
option

The combination of grains, vegetables and yummy sauces can never be exhausted, so spice up your life with turmeric, curry flavours and fresh ginger. For a gluten-free option, use rice, quinoa, millet or amaranth instead of barley.

Prep: 15 mins | Cook: 30 mins

2 teaspoons coconut oil, plus
2 tablespoons melted coconut oil

1 tablespoon cumin seeds

2 tablespoons minced fresh ginger

2 teaspoons turmeric

1 teaspoon coriander

¼ teaspoon cayenne

½ teaspoon sea salt

200 g (7 oz) barley

500 ml (18 fl oz) water

1 large sweet potato

1 large potato

3 parsnips

2 carrots

4 shallots

1 x Creamy Turmeric Dressing (page 59)

1 Heat 1 teaspoon of oil in a medium pan, add the cumin seeds and ginger and cook for 1 minute, until the seeds begin to pop. Add the turmeric, coriander, cayenne, salt, and stir. Add the barley and the water, bring to a boil, then cover and simmer for 20 minutes, or until the barley is tender and all the water has been absorbed. Fluff with a fork, cover, and set aside until the vegetables are ready.

2 Preheat the oven to 200°C (400°F). Peel and chop all vegetables into pieces of a similar size. Place in a roasting tin or baking dish, toss with the melted coconut oil and bake for 25 to 30 minutes, stirring once or twice, until the vegetables have softened and have begun to caramelise.

3 Place the cooked barley onto serving plates, and top with the root vegetables and dressing.

CALORIES (PER SERVING)	427
PROTEIN	10.4 G
TOTAL FAT	15.1 G
SATURATED FAT	8.8 G
CARBOHYDRATES	66.7 G
DIETARY FIBRE	14.6 G
SUGARS	5.8 G
VITAMINS	A

SAVOURY OATS WITH RED CABBAGE AND MUSHROOM

Serves 2
gluten-free
option

Oats are not only a breakfast food! Savoury oats make a great change to pasta night — and you get an extra helping of bone-strengthening manganese. For a gluten-free option, use gluten-free oats.

Prep: 5 mins | Cook: 15 mins

500 ml (18 fl oz) vegetable broth

90 g (3¼ oz) rolled oats

1 tablespoon coconut oil

2 garlic cloves, minced

10 cremini mushrooms, halved

140 g (4¾ oz) shredded red cabbage

1 avocado, sliced

sea salt and freshly ground black pepper, to taste

1 Bring the broth to a boil in a medium pot. Add the oats and stir. Reduce the heat to low and simmer for 15 to 20 minutes, stirring occasionally, until all the liquid has been absorbed.

2 Meanwhile, heat the oil over a medium heat in a frying pan and sauté the garlic, mushrooms and cabbage for 8 to 10 minutes, until the mushroom juices have cooked off. Season to taste.

3 Fold the sautéed vegetables into the cooked oats, and serve into bowls, topped with the avocado slices.

CALORIES (PER SERVING)	465
PROTEIN	9.3 G
TOTAL FAT	29.2 G
SATURATED FAT	10.5 G
CARBOHYDRATES	45.9 G
DIETARY FIBRE	13.9 G
SUGARS	5.8 G
VITAMINS	C

HEARTY SQUASH STEW WITH QUINOA

Serves 6–8
gluten-free

This stew is a real stick-to-your-ribs kind of recipe, perfect for a cold winter day. Quinoa thickens this one-pot meal while filling it with protein, fibre, iron, vitamin B6 and relaxing magnesium.

Prep: 15 mins | Cook: 40 mins

3 tablespoons coconut oil

1 onion, chopped

4 garlic cloves, minced

450 g (1 lb) butternut squash, cut into 5-cm (2-inch) cubes

3 Yukon Gold potatoes, cut into 5-cm (2-inch) cubes

1 x 800 g (28 oz) tin diced tomatoes

85 g (3 oz) quinoa

1 teaspoon chopped thyme

1 teaspoon chopped sage

250 ml (9 fl oz) water or vegetable broth

sea salt and freshly ground black pepper, to taste

1 Heat the oil in a large pot and sauté the onions and garlic for 3 to 4 minutes, until softened. Add the squash and potatoes and stir to coat in the oil. Cook for another 3 to 4 minutes, continuing to stir.

2 Add the tomatoes, quinoa, herbs, water or broth, 1 teaspoon of sea salt, and bring to a simmer. Cover and simmer for 30 minutes, stirring every 10 minutes. Season to taste, divide between serving bowls, and serve with crusty bread.

CALORIES (PER SERVING)	193
PROTEIN	4.6 G
TOTAL FAT	5.9 G
SATURATED FAT	4.5 G
CARBOHYDRATES	32.8 G
DIETARY FIBRE	5.8 G
SUGARS	6.2 G
VITAMINS	A, C

SWEET POTATO ROULADE WITH TOFU 'RICOTTA'

Serves 4–6
gluten-free

Try thinly sliced sweet potatoes in place of pasta in this roulade, and stuff them with tofu 'ricotta', my favourite protein-packed filling, which includes a nice helping of folate-rich spinach, too.

Prep: 35 mins | Cook: 15 mins

2 large sweet potatoes
extra-virgin olive oil
25 g (¾ oz) chopped toasted walnuts
chopped parsley, to serve

FOR THE FILLING

120 g (4¼ oz) spinach, roughly chopped
240 g (8¾ oz) firm or extra-firm tofu
3 tablespoons lemon juice
1 teaspoon nutritional yeast
sea salt and freshly ground black pepper, to taste

1 Peel each sweet potato and then slice off the ends and square off the four sides so that you end up with a block of potato. Carefully slice lengthways into 0.3-cm (⅛-inch) slices, ideally using a mandoline, though a sharp knife and steady hand will also work. If using a knife, it may be easier to build the dish as a lasagne (see variation).

2 Bring a pot of salted water to a boil over a medium heat, add 6 to 8 potato slices, and cook for 2 to 4 minutes, until tender but not mushy. Gently remove them from the water and place on a baking sheet to rest. Repeat with the remaining slices.

3 For the filling, lightly steam the spinach until wilted and reduced in bulk. In a food processor, combine the tofu, lemon juice and nutritional yeast, and process to combine, stopping to scrape down the sides as necessary. Season to taste, then transfer to a large bowl and fold in the spinach.

4 Preheat the oven to 180°C (350°F).

5 To assemble, coat a 23 x 33-cm (9 x 13-inch) baking dish with a little oil. Place 1 heaped tablespoon of filling on a slice of sweet potato and roll it up, placing it seam-side down in the dish. Repeat with the remaining filling and sweet potato slices. Drizzle the tops with olive oil, sprinkle over the walnuts, and bake for 15 minutes, until heated through. Top with the parsley and serve.

VARIATION: Create layers instead and build this as you would a lasagne. Bake it without a sauce, or use the sauce from the Spaghetti and Quinoa 'Meatballs' (page 118).

CALORIES (PER SERVING)	128
PROTEIN	5.5 G
TOTAL FAT	7.7 G
SATURATED FAT	1.1 G
CARBOHYDRATES	11.1 G
DIETARY FIBRE	2.6 G
SUGARS	2.4 G
VITAMINS	A, B6

POLENTA WITH KALE, PEPITAS AND POMEGRANATE

Braising your greens is a nice way to add flavour and make them a little more exciting, and I just love the addition of crunchy pumpkin seeds and tangy pomegranate arils.

Prep: 10 mins | Cook: 30 mins

Up to 1.75 litres (59 fl oz) water

225 g (8 oz) polenta

2 tablespoons nutritional yeast

¼ teaspoon smoked paprika

3 tablespoons extra-virgin olive oil

1 shallot, chopped

450 g (1 lb) kale leaves, woody stems removed (page 17)

250 ml (9 fl oz) vegetable broth

75 g (2½ oz) roasted pumpkin seeds

75 g (2½ oz) pomegranate arils (see tip, page 40)

sea salt and freshly ground black pepper, to taste

See image, opposite, front

1 Bring 1.5 litres (53 fl oz) of water to a boil in a medium pot. Pour in the polenta in a slow stream, whisking continuously until it is all added and the mixture is smooth. Stir until the polenta firms up, about 5 minutes. Reduce the heat to low, cover, and leave to cook for another 20 minutes, giving it a good stir every 5 minutes or so. The additional water can be added if the polenta becomes clumpy or difficult to stir. Remove from the heat and fold in the nutritional yeast and paprika.

2 In a large, deep pot, heat the oil and add the shallots, sautéing for 2 minutes, until fragrant. Add the kale leaves and the broth, a little at a time, allowing the kale to wilt before adding more. Once all the kale and broth have been added, cover and cook for 5 to 6 minutes, then remove the lid and cook off the liquid for another 2 minutes. Season to taste.

3 Divide the polenta between serving bowls and top with the braised kale, pumpkin seeds and pomegranate arils.

CALORIES (PER SERVING)	485
PROTEIN	15.2 G
TOTAL FAT	20.9 G
SATURATED FAT	3.3 G
CARBOHYDRATES	65.6 G
DIETARY FIBRE	8.2 G
SUGARS	3.6 G
VITAMINS	A, B6, C

CONFETTI SALAD
STUFFED PEPPERS

Serves 6
gluten-free

Stuffed peppers don't have to be boring – fill them with the bright, beautiful Goji Berry Confetti Salad (page 63) and enjoy a meal packed with nutritious veggies.

Prep: 25 mins | Cook: 20 mins

110–150 g (4–5 oz) cooked lentils or adzuki beans

1 x Goji Berry Confetti Salad (page 63)

6 peppers (yellow, orange, or red)

2 tablespoons Superfood Topper (page 55)

See image, page 135, rear

1 Preheat the oven to 180°C (350°F). In a large bowl, fold the cooked lentils or beans into the Goji Berry Confetti Salad.

2 Slice the tops off the peppers, reserving the stems. Carefully remove the core and inner membranes, then turn the peppers upside down, tapping the base to remove the seeds. Stand them upright in a baking dish – you may need to level them off on the bottoms slightly – and then spoon the salad mixture into each one, filling to the top. Top with the reserved stems and place 125 ml (4½ fl oz) of water in the base of the baking dish.

3 Bake for 20 minutes, until the peppers are fork tender. Remove the stems, sprinkle with the Superfood Topper, and serve with the stems in place.

CALORIES (PER SERVING)	347
PROTEIN	12.5 G
TOTAL FAT	13.5 G
SATURATED FAT	1.9 G
CARBOHYDRATES	46.1 G
DIETARY FIBRE	10.0 G
SUGARS	14.8 G
VITAMINS	A, C

VEGETABLE QUINOA 'FRIED RICE'

Forget takeaway: make this twist on fried rice in less time than it would take to have it delivered — especially if you use leftover quinoa.

Prep: 15 mins | Cook: 30 mins

170 g (5¾ oz) quinoa (or 550 g/ 1 lb 3½ oz leftover cooked quinoa)

500 ml (9 fl oz) water

1 tablespoon coconut oil

150 g (5 oz) diced onion

65 g (2¼ oz) diced carrot

50 g (1¾ oz) diced celery

90 g (3¼ oz) finely chopped broccoli florets and stems

2 tablespoons liquid aminos or gluten-free tamari

1 teaspoon five-spice powder

See image, page 139, rear

1 Rinse the quinoa well in a fine mesh sieve. In a small pan, bring the quinoa and water to a boil over a medium heat. Reduce the heat to low, cover, and simmer for 15 minutes, or until all the liquid has been absorbed. Remove from the heat and leave, covered, for an additional 5 minutes. Fluff with a fork and set aside.

2 Heat the oil in a wide frying pan and add the vegetables. Sauté over a medium-high heat for 5 minutes, until softened. Add the quinoa, liquid aminos and five-spice powder, and stir well. Continue to cook for 3 to 4 minutes, stirring often, then serve.

CALORIES (PER SERVING)	220
PROTEIN	7.4 G
TOTAL FAT	6.1 G
SATURATED FAT	3.2 G
CARBOHYDRATES	85.2 G
DIETARY FIBRE	5.2 G
SUGARS	2.9 G
VITAMINS	A, C

SPICY SPINACH COCONUT NOODLES

This is the perfect meal at the end of a long, hard day — you'll get greens and nuts and your dinner will be on the table in 15 minutes. For a gluten-free option, use 100% buckwheat noodles.

Prep: 10 mins | Cook: 10 mins

225 g (8 oz) soba noodles

250 ml (9 fl oz) light coconut milk

2 tablespoons almond butter (page 17)

1 tablespoon lime juice

2 tablespoons gluten-free tamari

2 teaspoons Sriracha or other chilli garlic sauce

180 g (6¼ oz) spinach, chopped

120 g (4¼ oz) toasted almonds, chopped

See image, opposite, front

1 Cook the noodles according to the packet instructions. Drain and set aside.

2 As the noodles are cooking, heat the coconut milk, almond butter, lime juice, tamari and Sriracha in a large frying pan over a low heat. Bring to a simmer and cook for 2 to 3 minutes, until slightly reduced. Add the spinach and cook for 2 minutes until tender, then add the cooked noodles and 85 g (3 oz) almonds, folding everything together and stirring well to coat with the sauce. Divide between plates, top with the remaining almonds, and serve with additional Sriracha and tamari at the table so the dish can be seasoned according to individual taste.

CALORIES (PER SERVING)	473
PROTEIN	18.4 G
TOTAL FAT	23.7 G
SATURATED FAT	4.8 G
CARBOHYDRATES	53.3 G
DIETARY FIBRE	5.1 G
SUGARS	1.5 G
VITAMINS	A

SUNFLOWER SEED AND SPROUT PAD THAI

Serves 4
gluten-free

A duo of sunflower seeds and sprouts provides bursts of linoleic acid (an essential fatty acid) and amino acids, including tryptophan – most commonly associated with turkey and post-Christmas dinner relaxation. This option is certainly more exciting, fresh and flavourful.

Prep: 15 mins | Cook: 15 mins

400 g (14 oz) flat rice noodles
1 tablespoon coconut oil
1 tablespoon minced fresh ginger
1 tablespoon minced garlic
1 large carrot, julienned
100 g (3½ oz) snow peas
75 g (2½ oz) toasted sunflower seeds
3 spring onions, thinly sliced
170 g (5¾ oz) sunflower sprouts
10 g (¼ oz) coriander, chopped, to serve
lime wedges, to serve

FOR THE SAUCE
60 ml (2 fl oz) lime juice
60 ml (2 fl oz) gluten-free tamari
60 ml (2 fl oz) water
1 tablespoon brown sugar
1–2 teaspoons chilli sauce, such as Sriracha

See image, opposite, front

1 Prepare the noodles according to the packet instructions and set aside.

2 Heat the oil in a large frying pan over a high heat. Add the ginger, garlic, carrots and snow peas, and cook, stirring continuously, for 2 minutes. Transfer to a bowl.

3 Return the pan to a medium-high heat and add the sauce ingredients, whisking to combine. Return the vegetables to the pan, with the noodles, sunflower seeds and spring onions, and stir to mix together and coat in the sauce. Cook for another 1 to 2 minutes. Remove from the heat, fold in the sunflower sprouts, and serve topped with coriander and lime wedges.

VARIATION: If sunflower sprouts aren't available, try using mung bean sprouts instead. Broccoli florets are another nice vegetable option instead of – or in addition to – the snow peas.

CALORIES (PER SERVING)	461
PROTEIN	10.7 G
TOTAL FAT	10.0 G
SATURATED FAT	3.4 G
CARBOHYDRATES	82.5 G
DIETARY FIBRE	4.4 G
SUGARS	4.8 G
VITAMINS	A

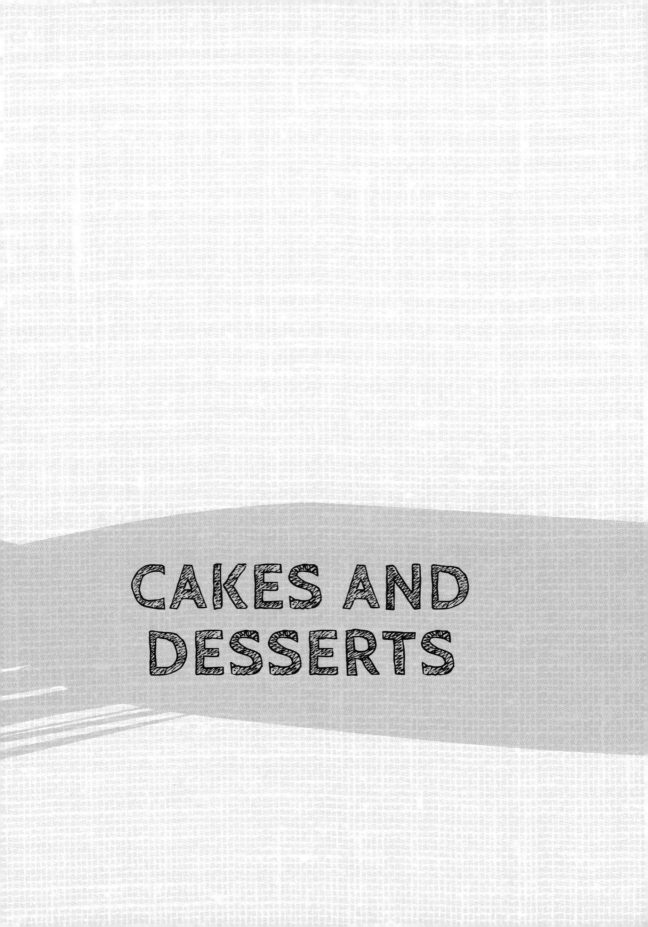

CAKES AND DESSERTS

RAW BROWNIE TRUFFLES

These truffles are one of my favourite indulgences. They have such a deep, rich flavour and they literally melt in your mouth. Sweetened only by dates, they're a healthy ending to any meal. Set a few aside to make the Quinoa Porridge (page 39).

Prep: 30 mins

100 g (3½ oz) walnuts
180 g (6¼ oz) medjool dates
40 g (1½ oz) cacao powder
¼ teaspoon sea salt

OPTIONAL GARNISHES

1 tablespoon cacao powder
1 tablespoon cacao nibs
1 tablespoon crushed pistachios mixed with 1 teaspoon matcha powder
*See image, opposite:
left, rear, with pistachios;
left, front, with cacao nibs;
right, rear, with cacao powder;
right, front, without garnish*

1 Line a plate with baking paper and set aside.

2 Pulse the walnuts in a food processor until they've broken down to a fine crumb (but before they turn to walnut butter). Add the dates, cacao powder and salt, and process until well combined. You may need to stop and scrape down the sides of the bowl. The dough should be soft and sticky enough to easily form a ball when rolled between your hands. If not, your dates may have been too dry, so add 1 teaspoon of water at a time until the dough is soft enough.

3 Scoop out a tablespoon of dough and roll it into a ball, then set it onto the plate. Repeat until all the dough is used up, then roll in a garnish of your choice, if desired, and place the balls in the freezer for 20 minutes. Remove from the freezer and serve; for a softer, fudgier truffle, leave to warm up for 15 minutes before serving. Transfer any leftovers to an airtight container and keep in the fridge or freezer for up to two weeks.

CALORIES (PER SERVING)	103
PROTEIN	3.2 G
TOTAL FAT	5.6 G
SATURATED FAT	0.7 G
CARBOHYDRATES	13.8 G
DIETARY FIBRE	2.6 G
SUGARS	9.7 G
VITAMINS	B6, E

ALMOND TAHINI TRUFFLES

Makes 12
gluten-free

These chocolate-covered truffles have a crunchy almond and creamy tahini filling — they remind me of a cross between Middle Eastern halva and Ferrero Rocher — and are a truly indulgent superfood treat.

Prep: 10 mins (plus freezing time)

170 g (5¾ oz) almonds
60 g (2 oz) tahini
2 tablespoons maple syrup
2 tablespoons ground flax meal
2 tablespoons coconut oil, softened
pinch of sea salt
75 g (2½ oz) vegan chocolate chips

1 Line a plate or baking sheet with baking paper and set aside. Place the almonds in a food processor and grind into a coarse flour.

2 In a bowl, mix three-quarters of the ground almonds with the tahini, maple syrup, flax meal, 1 tablespoon of the oil and the salt. Roll into 12 balls of equal size. Place the reserved ground almonds on a plate and roll each ball in them, pressing almond crumbs into the balls to make them stick. Place on the lined plate or sheet and freeze.

3 In a small pan, melt the chocolate chips with the remaining oil and stir until smooth. One at a time, dip each ball into the chocolate and roll it around to coat it. Return to the baking paper and repeat with the remaining balls. Place in the freezer to chill until set, about 5 to 10 minutes. Transfer to an airtight container and store in the freezer for up to two weeks.

VARIATION: Use almond butter (page 17) in place of the tahini for sweeter, nuttier truffles.

CALORIES (PER SERVING)	177
PROTEIN	4.6 G
TOTAL FAT	14.2 G
SATURATED FAT	4.0 G
CARBOHYDRATES	11.0 G
DIETARY FIBRE	2.6 G
SUGARS	2.6 G
VITAMINS	E

GOJI ALMOND ENERGY BITES

Makes 8–10
gluten-free
option

Raw snack bars are so delicious, but they can be expensive. It takes no time at all to make your own, and I love stocking my freezer with healthy, homemade energy bites for when hunger strikes. For a gluten-free option, use gluten-free oats.

Prep: 30 mins

30 g (1 oz) goji berries
170 g (5¾ oz) almonds
50 g (1¾ oz) rolled oats
pinch of sea salt
180 g (6¼ oz) medjool dates
2 tablespoons lemon juice

1 In a food processor fitted with the 'S' blade, pulse the goji berries until chopped (do not turn them into powder). Remove and set aside. Wipe out the bowl of the food processor.

2 Combine the almonds, oats and salt in the food processor and process until you get a fine crumb. Add the dates and 1 tablespoon of lemon juice and pulse until well combined. The dough should stick together when squeezed between your thumb and forefinger. If not, add the remaining tablespoon of lemon juice and pulse again. Add the gojis and pulse to incorporate.

3 Scoop out 2 teaspoons of the mixture and roll into a ball; you should be able to make 28 to 30 balls. Place them on a lined baking sheet and then put the sheet into the freezer for 20 minutes. Store the energy bites in an airtight container in the fridge or freezer for up to a month.

CALORIES (PER SERVING)	181
PROTEIN	5.0 G
TOTAL FAT	9.0 G
SATURATED FAT	0.7 G
CARBOHYDRATES	23.2 G
DIETARY FIBRE	4.3 G
SUGARS	14.6 G
VITAMINS	C, E

ADZUKI BEAN BROWNIES

Digging into a warm, two-bite vegan brownie is the best. Adzuki beans are soft with a sweet undertone, which is why they lend themselves so nicely to desserts, and they make these brownies extra fudgy.

Prep: 15 mins | Cook: 10 mins

1 x 400 g (14 oz) tin adzuki beans, drained and rinsed

40 g (1½ oz) cocoa or cacao powder

25 g (¾ oz) ground walnuts

60 ml (2 fl oz) melted coconut oil

100 g (3½ oz) coconut sugar or unrefined cane sugar

½ teaspoon bicarbonate of soda

½ teaspoon sea salt

¼ teaspoon cinnamon

2 flax eggs (page 17)

See image, opposite, rear

1 Preheat the oven to 180°C (350°F). Lightly grease a 24-hole mini muffin tin and set aside.

2 Place all the ingredients in a food processor and process until completely smooth, about 2 minutes, stopping to scrape down the sides of the bowl if necessary.

3 Scoop a heaped tablespoon of batter for each brownie into the prepared tin. Bake for 10 to 12 minutes, then remove from the oven and leave to cool in the pan for 5 minutes before transferring them to a cooling rack. Store in an airtight container for up to four days.

VARIATION: Use kidney beans or black beans as an alternative to adzuki beans.

CALORIES (PER SERVING)	90
PROTEIN	1.3 G
TOTAL FAT	3.5 G
SATURATED FAT	2.3 G
CARBOHYDRATES	14.5 G
DIETARY FIBRE	0.7 G
SUGARS	4.2 G
VITAMINS	B3, B6

LUCUMA ICE CREAM

Serves 4
gluten-free

This quick and easy recipe has only four ingredients and doesn't even require an ice cream maker. Lucuma is one of the most popular ice cream flavours in South America, and is amazing topped with cacao nib sprinkles and flaked sea salt.

Prep: 5 mins (plus 3 hrs' freezing)

1 x 400 ml (14 fl oz) tin full-fat coconut milk
65 g (2¼ oz) lucuma powder
3 tablespoons agave nectar
pinch of sea salt

See image, page 149, front

1 Place all the ingredients in a blender and blend for 2 minutes, until smooth.

2 Line a loaf tin with cling film and pour in the mix. Place in the freezer for 3 hours, or until firm and set. Remove 5 minutes before serving, to make it easier to scoop.

CALORIES (PER SERVING)	224
PROTEIN	2.1 G
TOTAL FAT	12.0 G
SATURATED FAT	8.0 G
CARBOHYDRATES	26.6 G
DIETARY FIBRE	0.5 G
SUGARS	12.2 G
VITAMINS	B3, C

THREE-INGREDIENT CHIA PUDDING

Serves 2
gluten-free

One of the incredible qualities of the tiny chia seeds is an ability to absorb a huge amount of liquid. When they do this, they become plump and gelatinous, making for an easy and yummy pudding that comes with a little 'pop'!

Prep: 5 mins (plus 2–8 hrs' to set)

250 ml (9 fl oz) unsweetened almond milk (or other non-dairy milk)
1 tablespoon agave nectar
40 g (1½ oz) chia seeds

See image, opposite, rear

1 In a large bowl or jar, combine the milk, agave and chia. Leave for 5 minutes, then stir (or shake if using a jar) again. Place in the fridge for at least 2 hours, or overnight. Remove from the fridge, stir, then serve.

VARIATIONS: For a chocolate chia pudding, add 2 tablespoons cacao powder and a pinch of sea salt to the mix.

CALORIES (PER SERVING)	114
PROTEIN	4.5 G
TOTAL FAT	7.9 G
SATURATED FAT	0.5 G
CARBOHYDRATES	14.2 G
DIETARY FIBRE	7.5 G
SUGARS	5.4 G
VITAMINS	A, B1, B3

COCONUT MILK MATCHA PUDDING

This rich and luxurious pudding relies on potent matcha tea for its gorgeous green hue and energy- and mood-boosting properties. The strength of the matcha is complemented beautifully by the creaminess of the coconut.

Prep: 5 mins | Cook: 15 mins (plus 1 hr to set)

1 x 400 ml (14 fl oz) tin full-fat coconut milk

65 g (2¼ oz) coconut sugar or unrefined cane sugar

2 teaspoons matcha powder

pinch of sea salt

1 tablespoon cornflour

cacao nibs or shaved dark chocolate, to serve

See image, page 151, front

1 Place 375 ml (13 fl oz) coconut milk in a small pan along with the sugar, matcha powder and salt, whisking to combine. Heat to a gentle simmer over a medium heat, stirring occasionally, for about 5 minutes.

2 While the milk is heating, whisk together the remaining coconut milk and cornflour in a bowl until no lumps remain.

3 Add the cornflour mixture to the pan and whisk until smooth, bringing it back to a simmer. Cook until the mixture begins to thicken, about 5 minutes, then reduce the heat to low and continue to stir for another 2 minutes.

4 Transfer to individual bowls or ramekins, cover with cling film that touches the surface of the pudding (to prevent a skin from forming), and place in the fridge to set for an hour. Remove the cling film, top with cacao nibs or shaved chocolate, and enjoy.

VARIATION: If you find the flavour of matcha too strong, try stirring 60 ml (2 fl oz) of melted dark chocolate into the pudding while it's still warm.

CALORIES (PER SERVING)	140
PROTEIN	1.0 G
TOTAL FAT	12.0 G
SATURATED FAT	8.0 G
CARBOHYDRATES	7.2 G
DIETARY FIBRE	0.6 G
SUGARS	2.3 G
VITAMINS	C

GOJI CHIP CAKE

Serves 8
(makes 1 x
3-tier cake)

When I was growing up, I always requested a cherry-chip cake for my birthday. This recipe satisfies my nostalgia without compromising my health — instead of using synthetic 'fruit' pieces, I add vibrant chopped goji berries.

Prep: 20 mins | Cook: 25 mins

250 ml (9 fl oz) unsweetened non-dairy milk (of choice)

1 tablespoon apple cider vinegar

85 ml (3 fl oz) vegetable oil (canola, safflower, etc.)

½ teaspoon almond extract

30 g (1 oz) goji berries

190 g (6¾ oz) plain flour

150 g (5 oz) unrefined cane sugar

1 teaspoon baking powder

½ teaspoon bicarbonate of soda

¼ teaspoon sea salt

FOR THE ICING

125 ml (4½ fl oz) coconut oil

250 g (9 oz) vegan icing sugar

2 tablespoons non-dairy milk (of choice)

See image, page 142

1 Preheat the oven to 180°C (350°F). Prepare three 12-cm (5-inch) cake tins (or a single 20-cm/8-inch cake tin, if preferred) by greasing the sides and lining the bottoms with a circle of baking paper.

2 In a large bowl, combine the milk and vinegar and allow to curdle, about 2 minutes. Add the oil and almond extract and mix together.

3 Pulse the goji berries in a food processor until roughly chopped, and set aside. Into a separate bowl, sift the flour, sugar, baking powder, bicarbonate of soda and salt, and stir to combine. Add the dry ingredients to the wet ingredients and mix until just combined and no lumps remain. Then fold the goji berries into the batter.

4 Divide the batter evenly between the cake tins and bake for 22 to 25 minutes, or until a skewer inserted into the cakes comes out clean. Remove from the oven and allow to cool fully before removing from the tins.

5 For the icing, cream the coconut oil in a stand mixer or with a handheld mixer until smooth and fluffy. Add 125 g (4½ oz) of sugar and mix again to incorporate. Add the second cup and mix again, adding a tablespoon or two of milk to achieve a fluffy icing.

6 Using a serrated knife, carefully slice the domed tops off each cooled cake. Place one cake on the plate or cake stand on which you'll be serving it. Spread one-third of the icing on top, all the way out to the edges. Top with the second cake and another one-third of the icing. Top with the final cake and finish with the remaining icing. Coconut oil icing does not hold up well in the heat (or even at room temperature), so keep the cake refrigerated until ready to serve.

CALORIES (PER SERVING)	513
PROTEIN	2.7 G
TOTAL FAT	25.2 G
SATURATED FAT	13.2 G
CARBOHYDRATES	71.6 G
DIETARY FIBRE	1.1 G
SUGARS	50.6 G
VITAMINS	C

MORNING GLORY MUFFINS

Makes 12

Carrot, apple, coconut, pumpkin, raisins, nuts — these muffins are packing enough to fuel you through the toughest of morning snacking emergencies.

Prep: 30 mins | Cook: 25 mins

250 g (9 oz) whole-wheat flour

2 teaspoons baking powder

1 teaspoon cinnamon

¼ teaspoon nutmeg

¼ teaspoon sea salt

125 ml (4½ fl oz) sunflower or canola oil, plus a little extra for spraying

150 g (5 oz) brown sugar

125 ml (4½ fl oz) non-dairy milk (of choice)

220 g (7¾ oz) pumpkin purée (page 17) or tinned pumpkin

35 g (1¼ oz) grated carrot

35 g (1¼ oz) grated apple

35 g (1¼ oz) chopped walnuts

25 g (¾ oz) unsweetened desiccated coconut

60 g (2 oz) raisins or cranberries

1 Preheat the oven to 200°C (400°F). Spray a 12-hole muffin tin with oil, or line with silicone or muffin cases.

2 In a large bowl, mix together the flour, baking powder, spices and salt. Set aside.

3 In another large bowl, mix together the oil, sugar, milk and pumpkin purée. Add the carrot and apple and stir to combine. Add the dry ingredients and mix until just combined. Fold in the walnuts, coconut and raisins or cranberries.

4 Scoop the batter into the prepared muffin tin, filling each hole almost to the top. Bake for 25 minutes, or until a skewer inserted into a muffin comes out clean. Leave to cool, then store in an airtight container for up to four days, or freeze.

CALORIES (PER SERVING)	269
PROTEIN	4.1 G
TOTAL FAT	14.1 G
SATURATED FAT	2.4 G
CARBOHYDRATES	34.9 G
DIETARY FIBRE	4.1 G
SUGARS	16.5 G
VITAMINS	A

BLUEBERRY BUCKWHEAT BARS

These delicious, versatile bars are great for dessert with a scoop of non-dairy ice cream, but you can also serve them as a sweet afternoon snack. For a gluten-free option, use gluten-free oats.

Prep: 20 mins | Cook: 35 mins

290 g (10¼ oz) blueberries, fresh or frozen
60 ml (2 fl oz) orange juice
2 tablespoons maple syrup
2 tablespoons chia seeds
210 g (7¼ oz) buckwheat groats
140 g (4¾ oz) rolled oats
2 tablespoons lucuma powder
2 tablespoons brown sugar
½ teaspoon cinnamon
¼ teaspoon sea salt
¼ teaspoon bicarbonate of soda
2 flax eggs (page 17)
3 tablespoons melted coconut oil
2 tablespoons water
See image, page 158, rear

1 Preheat the oven to 180°C (350°F). Line a 20 x 20-cm (8 x 8-inch) baking dish with baking paper.

2 In a small pan, simmer the blueberries, orange juice and maple syrup over a low heat for 5 to 7 minutes, until the blueberry juices begin to release. Stir in the chia seeds and simmer for another 2 minutes, stirring until it thickens a little. Remove from the heat and set aside.

3 Combine 170 g (5¾ oz) buckwheat groats with all the remaining ingredients in a food processor and process to a coarse crumble. Add the remaining 40 g (1½ oz) buckwheat and pulse to combine.

4 Place two-thirds of the crumble in the baking dish and press firmly into an even layer. Top with the blueberries and spread out to cover the base. Scatter the remaining crumble on top of the blueberries.

5 Bake for 30 to 35 minutes, then remove from the oven and leave to cool fully before slicing in the pan.

CALORIES (PER SERVING)	226
PROTEIN	5.3 G
TOTAL FAT	7.2 G
SATURATED FAT	4.3 G
CARBOHYDRATES	36.3 G
DIETARY FIBRE	4.9 G
SUGARS	9.0 G
VITAMINS	B6

NO-BAKE QUINOA CEREAL BARS

Makes 8
gluten-free

These bars are the perfect healthy grab-and-go snack, ideal for a journey or a day of errands. I like to use apple-juice-sweetened cranberries as I find others too sweet.

Prep: 30 mins

75 g (2½ oz) crisp brown rice cereal

50 g (1¾ oz) puffed quinoa cereal

75 g (2½ oz) raw pumpkin seeds

35 g (1¼ oz) shelled hemp seeds

30 g (1 oz) dried cranberries

3 tablespoons ground flax meal

170 ml (5¾ fl oz) brown rice syrup

125 g (4½ oz) peanut butter

1 teaspoon vanilla extract

See image, page 158, right

1 Line a 20 x 20-cm (8 x 8-inch) baking dish with baking paper and set aside.

2 In a large bowl, combine the cereals, seeds, cranberries and flax meal. Set aside.

3 In a small pan, heat the brown rice syrup and peanut butter over a medium-low heat until melted and stir until smooth, about 2 to 3 minutes. Remove from the heat and stir in the vanilla extract. Pour over the cereal and mix together, being sure to coat everything. Transfer to the prepared dish and press it down evenly, using a spatula or damp hands (to prevent sticking). Leave for 20 minutes at room temperature, or 5 minutes in the freezer, to set.

4 Slice into eight bars and serve. Store any remaining bars in an airtight container; if you'll be enjoying them on the go, wrap each bar individually in baking paper.

SUPERFOOD TIP: For a nut-free option, try these with sunflower seed butter in place of the peanut butter.

CALORIES (PER SERVING)	266
PROTEIN	9.8 G
TOTAL FAT	15.4 G
SATURATED FAT	2.6 G
CARBOHYDRATES	27.5 G
DIETARY FIBRE	2.8 G
SUGARS	14.4 G
VITAMINS	B6

BAKED ALMOND GRANOLA BARS

With a growing toddler at home who's always on the go, I try to stock my kitchen (and bag) with healthy snacks. These granola bars are full of protein and iron for growing minds and bodies. For a gluten-free option, use gluten-free rolled oats.

Prep: 10 mins | Cook: 35 mins

140 g (4¾ oz) rolled oats

85 g (3 oz) almonds, chopped

100 g (3½ oz) dried apricots, chopped (optional)

25 g (¾ oz) unsweetened desiccated coconut

3 tablespoons oat flour

60 ml (2 fl oz) agave nectar or maple syrup

60 ml (2 fl oz) melted coconut oil

2 tablespoons chia seeds

½ teaspoon cinnamon

¼ teaspoon salt

See image, opposite, front

1 Preheat the oven to 180°C (350°F). Line a 20 x 20-cm (8 x 8-inch) baking dish with baking paper.

2 Lightly toast the oats and almonds by spreading them out on a baking sheet and placing them in the oven for 5 minutes.

3 In a large bowl, mix together the rolled oats, almonds, apricots (if using), coconut and the oat flour.

4 In a smaller bowl, combine the agave or maple syrup, coconut oil, chia seeds, cinnamon and salt. Add this to the dry ingredients and stir well to combine.

5 Pour into the prepared baking dish and spread into an even layer, pressing firmly to pack down the mixture. Bake for 30 to 35 minutes, until golden brown. Remove from the oven and leave the bars to cool completely before cutting. Store the bars in an airtight container; if you'll be enjoying them on the go, wrap each bar individually.

SUPERFOOD TIP: You can make your own oat flour quickly and easily by grinding rolled oats in your blender or food processor.

CALORIES (PER SERVING)	201
PROTEIN	4.4 G
TOTAL FAT	13.4 G
SATURATED FAT	7.2 G
CARBOHYDRATES	18.4 G
DIETARY FIBRE	3.7 G
SUGARS	5.1 G
VITAMINS	A, E

MINTY MATCHA NANAIMO BARS

Makes 25
gluten-free

Nanaimo bars are a quintessential Canadian treat. Named after the town from which they originate, they are rich slices of goodness, with a chocolate and coconut base, a creamy filling, and topped with raw chocolate.

Prep: 40 mins

FOR THE BASE

50 g (1¾ oz) walnuts

85 g (3 oz) almonds

180 g (6¼ oz) medjool dates

3 tablespoons cacao powder

25 g (¾ oz) unsweetened desiccated coconut

pinch of sea salt

FOR THE MIDDLE LAYER

225 g (8 oz) unsweetened desiccated coconut

3 tablespoons agave nectar or maple syrup

2 tablespoons coconut oil

½ teaspoon pure mint extract

2 teaspoons matcha powder

FOR THE TOP LAYER

1 x Easy Raw Maca Chocolate Bark (without the toppings) (page 164)

1 Line a 20 x 20-cm (8 x 8-inch) baking dish with baking paper and set aside.

2 For the base, grind the walnuts and almonds in a food processor until the consistency of a coarse flour. Add the remaining ingredients and process until broken down; when pinched between your thumb and forefinger the mixture should stick together. If not, add a tablespoon of water and try again. Transfer to the baking dish and press down firmly in an even layer. Place in the freezer.

3 For the middle layer, wipe out the bowl of the food processor. Add the desiccated coconut and process until it turns into coconut butter, about 4 to 5 minutes. Then add the remaining ingredients and process to combine. Add this layer on top of the base layer and smooth out with a spatula or the back of a spoon. Return to the freezer.

4 Make a batch of the Easy Raw Maca Chocolate Bark (page 164) and add this to the dish as the final layer, smoothing it out with a spatula or the back of a spoon. Return to the freezer for 20 minutes.

5 Slice into 16 bars using a heated knife to cut through without breaking the chocolate layer. Store in an airtight container in the fridge or freezer for up to two weeks. If storing in the freezer, remove 20 minutes before serving (10 minutes if storing in the fridge).

CALORIES (PER SERVING)	196
PROTEIN	2.8 G
TOTAL FAT	16.0 G
SATURATED FAT	11.3 G
CARBOHYDRATES	14.9 G
DIETARY FIBRE	4.1 G
SUGARS	9.2 G
VITAMINS	B6, E

LEMON CHIA 'POPPYSEED' LOAF

Serves 8–10

This scrumptious lemon cake doesn't actually have any poppyseeds in it — instead, chia seeds fill in, offering a crunchy pop as well as omega-3s and dietary fibre.

Prep: 10 mins | Cook: 40 mins

juice and zest of 2 lemons
140 g (4¾ oz) unrefined cane sugar
65 g (2¼ oz) unsweetened apple sauce
60 ml (2 fl oz) sunflower oil (or canola, coconut, etc.)
250 g (9 oz) plain flour
2 teaspoons baking powder
½ teaspoon turmeric
¼ teaspoon bicarbonate of soda
¼ teaspoon fine sea salt
3 tablespoons chia seeds
30 g (1 oz) vegan icing sugar

1 Preheat the oven to 180°C (350°F). Lightly grease a loaf tin, or line with baking paper, and set aside.

2 In a large bowl, combine a scant 125 ml (4½ fl oz) of lemon juice, the lemon zest, sugar, apple sauce and oil.

3 Place all the dry ingredients, except the icing sugar, in another bowl and stir to combine. Add the dry ingredients to the wet and stir until just mixed.

4 Transfer the batter to the prepared tin and bake for 35 to 45 minutes, or until a skewer inserted into the cake comes out clean. Remove from the oven and allow to cool fully before removing from the tin.

5 Whisk together the icing sugar and 1 tablespoon of lemon juice until smooth. Drizzle over the loaf, slice, and serve.

CALORIES (PER SERVING)	222
PROTEIN	3.1 G
TOTAL FAT	7.0 G
SATURATED FAT	0.7 G
CARBOHYDRATES	37.2 G
DIETARY FIBRE	1.6 G
SUGARS	16.7 G
VITAMINS	C

EASY RAW MACA CHOCOLATE BARK

You won't believe how easy it is to make your own superfood chocolate. Raw cacao powder has a potent antioxidant power, while maca gives an extra kick of mood-enhancing chemicals, but the beauty of this chocolate is in the superfood toppings.

Prep: 20 mins

125 ml (4½ fl oz) melted coconut oil
60 ml (2 fl oz) agave nectar
65 g (2¼ oz) cacao powder
2 tablespoons maca powder
¼ teaspoon sea salt
1 tablespoon goji berries
1 tablespoon cacao nibs
1 tablespoon pumpkin seeds

1 Line a small baking sheet with baking paper.

2 Whisk together the coconut oil and agave in a bowl until completely mixed. Add the cacao powder, maca powder and salt, whisking continuously until smooth. Work quickly as the mixture will start to solidify.

3 Pour the chocolate onto the baking paper, using a spatula to get every last bit from the bowl, and top with goji berries, cacao nibs and pumpkin seeds. Place in the freezer to set for 20 minutes. Break into pieces and enjoy immediately. Store any remaining chocolate in the freezer.

VARIATION: For a Mexican-style version, add ½ teaspoon of cinnamon and ¼ teaspoon of cayenne to the chocolate mix and top with pieces of chopped crystallised ginger.

CALORIES (PER SERVING)	218
PROTEIN	2.8 G
TOTAL FAT	18.7 G
SATURATED FAT	15.1 G
CARBOHYDRATES	14.2 G
DIETARY FIBRE	4.5 G
SUGARS	7.2 G
VITAMINS	B2, B3, B6, C

DOUBLE CHOCOLATE LENTIL COOKIES

Makes 24

It's no secret: I like to put pulses in my desserts. It adds an extra protein and fibre punch, and if I can have a cookie that does that, I'm happy. Don't miss out on eating one warm from the oven.

Prep: 25 mins | Cook: 10–12 mins

100 g (3½ oz) red lentils, rinsed
500 ml (18 fl oz) water
125 ml (4½ fl oz) coconut oil, softened
100 g (3½ oz) unrefined cane sugar
190 g (6¾ oz) plain flour
40 g (1½ oz) cocoa or cacao powder
1 teaspoon bicarbonate of soda
½ teaspoon sea salt
50 g (1¾ oz) vegan chocolate chips

See image, page 166, rear

1 Preheat the oven to 180°C (350°F). Line two baking sheets with baking paper.

2 Place the lentils and water in a small pan over a medium heat and bring to a boil. Reduce the heat to low and simmer for 20 minutes, until tender. Drain, then measure out 75 g (2½ oz) cooked lentils, transfer to a large bowl and mash with a fork. Add the oil and sugar to the mashed lentils and cream together.

3 In a separate bowl, combine the flour, cocoa or cacao powder, bicarbonate of soda and sea salt. Add to the lentil mixture and stir to incorporate. Fold in the chocolate chips.

4 The dough will be quite sticky, but scoop out 1 heaped tablespoon at a time and roll into balls. Place the balls on the prepared sheets and flatten gently with your hand. Bake for 10 to 12 minutes. Remove from the oven and allow to cool for 5 minutes on the sheets before transferring to a cooling rack.

CALORIES (PER SERVING)	120
PROTEIN	2.4 G
TOTAL FAT	6.2 G
SATURATED FAT	5.0 G
CARBOHYDRATES	14.8 G
DIETARY FIBRE	2.1 G
SUGARS	5.5 G
VITAMINS	B1, B6

CHAI-SPICED COCONUT MACAROONS

Makes 12

These crunchy, domed coconut cookies are not too sweet and are lightly flavoured with cinnamon and chai spices. They're full of iron, dietary fibre and healthy fats — a great superfood cookie!

Prep: 10 mins | Cook: 30 mins

170 g (5¾ oz) almonds
120 g (4¼ oz) unsweetened desiccated coconut
60 ml (2 fl oz) coconut oil, softened
2 tablespoons lucuma powder
1 teaspoon cardamom powder
1 teaspoon cinnamon
½ teaspoon ginger powder
⅛ teaspoon white pepper (optional)
pinch of cloves
60 ml (2 fl oz) brown rice syrup
⅛ teaspoon sea salt

1 Preheat the oven to 120°C (250°F). Line a baking sheet with baking paper.

2 Place the almonds and coconut in a food processor and grind to a coarse flour. Add the remaining ingredients and process to combine, about 15 to 20 seconds.

3 Using a 14 g (0.5 oz) ice cream scoop or rounded tablespoon, scoop the cookie batter into rounds with flattened bottoms and place on the prepared sheet. They need to be really tightly packed to ensure they don't crumble apart after baking. Bake for 25 to 30 minutes, until lightly browned. Allow to cool on the baking sheet before transferring to an airtight container for storage.

VARIATION: Take these cookies over the top by adding a chocolate dip. Melt 75 g (2½ oz) of vegan chocolate chips with 1 teaspoon of coconut oil. Dip the bottom third of each macaroon into it and transfer to a piece of baking paper to set. Alternatively, you can dip them into the Easy Raw Maca Chocolate Bark (page 164), but as it's not stable at room temperature, the cookies would then need to be stored in the freezer.

CALORIES (PER SERVING)	212
PROTEIN	4.0 G
TOTAL FAT	18.3 G
SATURATED FAT	10.4 G
CARBOHYDRATES	11.4 G
DIETARY FIBRE	3.5 G
SUGARS	4.6 G
VITAMINS	B3, E

SWEET POTATO 'CHEESECAKE'

Sweet potato is often overlooked when it comes to dessert, but just like pumpkin it makes a great purée with natural sweetness. This 'cheesecake' is rich and creamy with a lovely flavour, but don't be fooled — it doesn't contain any cheese!

Prep: 20 mins | Cook: 15 mins (plus 6–8 hrs' freezing)

FOR THE CRUST

85 g (3 oz) pecans

30 g (1 oz) rolled oats

2 tablespoons maple syrup

60 ml (2 fl oz) coconut oil

½ teaspoon cinnamon

FOR THE FILLING

1 x 350 g (12 oz) packet silken tofu

170 g (5¾ oz) raw cashews, soaked for 4 hours

60 ml (2 fl oz) lemon juice

250 g (9 oz) mashed sweet potato

125 ml (4½ fl oz) melted coconut oil

75 g (2½ oz) brown sugar or coconut sugar

2 teaspoons vanilla extract

1 teaspoon cinnamon

1 For the crust, preheat the oven to 180°C (350°F). Place the pecans and oats in a food processor and process to a coarse flour. Add the maple syrup, coconut oil and cinnamon, and pulse to combine. The mixture should stick together when pressed between the thumb and forefinger; if not, add a tablespoon of water and try again. Press into an 18-cm (7-inch) springform tin and bake for 10 to 15 minutes, until lightly browned. Wipe down the food processor bowl.

2 Place all the filling ingredients in the food processor and process until smooth, stopping to scrape down the sides as necessary.

3 Pour the filling into the springform tin on top of the crust. Smooth out with a spatula or the back of a spoon. Transfer to the freezer for at least 6 hours, ideally overnight, to set. Transfer to the fridge at least 1 to 2 hours prior to serving – unless it's a hot summer's day, in which case a frozen slice of cheesecake would be amazing!

CALORIES (PER SERVING)	422
PROTEIN	7.7 G
TOTAL FAT	34.3 G
SATURATED FAT	18.4 G
CARBOHYDRATES	25.1 G
DIETARY FIBRE	2.9 G
SUGARS	11.2 G
VITAMINS	A, B6, C

SUPERFOOD HOT CHOCOLATE

Serves 2
gluten-free

This thick hot chocolate is spiked with warming spices like cinnamon, cayenne and ginger — perfect for thawing out by the fire after spending time in the cold.

Prep: 5 mins (plus 3 hrs' freezing)

2 tablespoons cacao powder

2 tablespoons coconut sugar or unrefined cane sugar

60 ml (2 fl oz) water

1 teaspoon maca powder

½ teaspoon cinnamon

⅛ teaspoon cayenne

⅛ teaspoon ginger powder

pinch of sea salt

1 teaspoon coconut oil

500 ml (18 fl oz) non-dairy milk (of choice)

1 Place all the ingredients in a blender and blend until smooth, about 1 minute.

2 Pour the contents into a small pan and heat gently over a medium heat for 6 to 8 minutes. Pour into cups and enjoy.

CALORIES (PER SERVING)	181
PROTEIN	2.7 G
TOTAL FAT	7.7 G
SATURATED FAT	2.6 G
CARBOHYDRATES	27.7 G
DIETARY FIBRE	3.4 G
SUGARS	20.9 G
VITAMINS	A

GOLDEN TURMERIC MILK

Serves 2
gluten-free

Golden milk is a traditional Ayurvedic beverage that utilises the healing power of turmeric. This warm, soothing milk is especially nice in the evening as you relax.

Prep: 5 mins | **Cook**: 5 mins

500 ml (18 fl oz) non-dairy milk (of choice)

1 teaspoon turmeric or 1 tablespoon minced fresh turmeric

¼ teaspoon ginger powder or ½ teaspoon minced fresh ginger

¼ teaspoon cinnamon

pinch of black pepper

1 teaspoon coconut oil

maple syrup, to taste

1 Place all the ingredients, except the maple syrup, in a small pan and heat gently for 10 minutes, but do not bring to a boil. Sweeten to taste with maple syrup, strain through a fine mesh sieve (if using fresh turmeric or ginger), and serve.

CALORIES (PER SERVING)	111
PROTEIN	1.2 G
TOTAL FAT	6.8 G
SATURATED FAT	2.0 G
CARBOHYDRATES	11.1 G
DIETARY FIBRE	1.5 G
SUGARS	7.5 G
VITAMINS	A

GENERAL INDEX

RECIPE INDEX

CREDITS
Quantum Publishing would like to thank the following for supplying images for inclusion in this book:

8: marekuliasz/Shutterstock.com; 10: Elena M. Tarasova/Shutterstock.com; 11: wanchai/ Shutterstock.com; 12: Dionisvera/Shutterstock. com; 14: Africa Studio/Shutterstock.com; 15: panda3800/Shutterstock.com; 16: antpkr/ Shutterstock.com

All other images are the copyright of Quantum Publishing. All other photography by Jackie Sobon.

While every effort has been made to credit contributors, Quantum Publishing would like to apologise should there have been any omissions or errors and would be pleased to make the appropriate correction to future editions of the book.

RESOURCES

WHERE TO FIND SUPERFOODS
It's becoming so much easier to source the various superfoods detailed in this book – after all, they are for the most part fruits, vegetables, nuts, seeds and pulses. For the less well-known ingredients, the best places to start are health food shops and larger supermarkets. Many shops now have natural foods sections where you can find shelled hemp seeds, coconut oil, chia seeds, and so on.

LARGER SUPERMARKETS AND INDEPENDENT SHOPS
If there's an organic food or superfood on the market, there's a good chance you'll be able to find it at your nearest large supermarket or any big fruit and vegetable supplier, such as a farmers market.

HEALTH FOOD SHOPS
These speciality shops are great – staff are usually very knowledgeable and can often source those 'hard to find' ingredients. I shop at my local health food shop for raw cacao, goji berries, organic turmeric, and matcha, among other things.

ONLINE
When all else fails, you can always seek out that elusive ingredient online. There are many websites that stock superfoods and dried goods travel very well.

ACKNOWLEDGEMENTS

This book wasn't created by my hand alone, and I would like to express my gratitude for the support of the following amazing individuals for their contributions.

To the team at Quantum, my thanks are many: Kerry Enzor, Sorrel Wood and Emma Harverson, thank you for your amazing work in managing the project, and to Hazel Eriksson for getting the book up and running. Lucy Parissi, thank you for your beautiful design and layout. Rachel Malig, my editor extraordinaire, thank you for sifting through my words and thoughts and helping me make sense of it all.

To the team at The Experiment, my thanks to you: most notably Matthew Lore, Allie Bochicchio, Jennifer Hergenroeder, Dan O'Connor, Sarah Smith, Sarah Schneider, Karen Giangreco and Sasha Tropp.

Jackie Sobon, once again your visual imagery is astounding and mouth-wateringly beautiful. I am so very grateful to have had your time and energy dedicated to bringing my recipes to life on the page. Well done, madame.

Thank you to my many recipe testers who came out in droves to offer their time tirelessly. This time my crew of helpers included friends, acquaintances, relatives of old camp friends, even people I went to high school with, which made the whole process that much more special. To the new friends made along the way: Kim Logan, Kate Finman, Laura Thompson, Barbara Davidge, Jennifer Elfenbein, Alex Wurtele, Tammy Root, Diana Carruthers, Lisa Colvin, Erika Rostron. To my Sudbury crew: Tara Levesque, Leanne Morin, Ty Cumming, Josée Cyr, Krista McDonald, Monique Beaudoin. To my mama tribe: Katie Bisset, Chrystal Robertson, Erin Ethelston, Lynn Despatie. And to my best friends since forever: Susan Cass, Andrea Lane.

Thank you to my parents, Laurie and Joe, for your love, support, and for telling everyone you meet that I'm a published author, along with the other well-meaning grassroots publicity work you do. You're both hilarious and I love you. To the rest of my family and friends, and everyone who has chipped in along the way, you continue to rally your support for me and I can't thank you enough.

Woodrow, thank you for being the sweet, spirited child that you are. You make every day a super adventure and I look forward to watching you as you continue to grow into a loving and compassionate boy. Also, your cookie taste-testing abilities are top notch.

Mark, thank you for your endless love and partnership and for helping me carve out time for writing, even though you were simultaneously in the process of opening a restaurant. Your drive to change the world is inspiring and I'm so lucky to share this journey with you.

Finally, thank you to my Cupcakes and Kale readers and the many vegan bloggers and authors who continue to inspire me with their work. What an amazing community, built around love and compassion for all.